SECURE SUCCESS

STACI D. HUDDLESTON

SECURE SUCCESS

SECURE SUCCESS

A PROVEN PLAN TO PROSPERING PERSONALLY & PROFESSIONALLY

STACI D. HUDDLESTON

SECURE SUCCESS

For information contact:

email: Staci.D.Huddleston@gmail.com

website: https://StaciHuddleston.com

Cover design by Designer Umair Tariq

Hardcover ISBN: 978-1-7352581-0-2

Paperback ISBN: 978-1-7352581-2-6

eBook ISBN: 978-1-7352581-1-9

First Edition: December 2020

DEDICATION

I dedicate this book to everyone who has ever wanted more but has been told time and time again that more was not within their reach; for those who struggle to find the inspiration they need to be all that they can be while smiling in the faces of all who doubted them as they pass them by on the way to the top. A boss I admire once told me it's lonely at the top, but what I'll tell you is that it's only lonely at the top if you fail to build sustaining relationships on your way up and fail to continue to nurture them once you get there.

TABLE OF CONTENTS

Dedication..........v
Table Of Contents..........vi
Acknowledgements..........viii
PROSPERING PERSONALLY..........xi
Introduction..........1
Self..........15
Mind..........21
Body..........35
Soul..........63
Financial..........77
PROSPERING PROFESSIONALLY..........129
Securing Skills..........131

Professional Development 149

PROSPERING PERSONALLY & PROFESSIONALLY....................163

'Ships 165

Goals....................185

Passion, Purpose, & Prosperity 201

Networking....................215

Branding....................225

Style 233

Service 259

Summary....................271

Bibliography....................278

About The Author 282

ACKNOWLEDGEMENTS

I have to start by thanking my mother, Deiadra Criggler-Lewis who is always super supportive of everything that I do. Thanks to my father, Brice Huddleston III, and my stepfather, Charles Lewis Jr., for being supportive, loving, and showing me what hard-working good, Godly men are. Thank you to my little sister, Cayci Lewis, and my friend, Tiffany Currie-Jones, who were the first readers of my original work on my first fictional novel that I put on hold for this book which is more in line with my purpose. I will finish that book one day, but it is my hope that this book is an inspiration to others. My sister, Tiffany Huddleston, I thank you for giving me the courage to do anything. I don't think that you have ever thought that there was anything you couldn't do and that is one of the qualities I admire most about you; thanks for helping me to see that if I can dream it I can achieve it. To all the amazing women in my family and inner circle who show me each and every day what it's like to succeed at whatever they put their minds to and in every area of their lives: I thank you, Dr. Nikkya Coleman-Lewis, Dr. Andrea'netta Mechelle Haywood, Montrice Dye, Leah Hendricks, Dana Burge-Watson, and Shontel Hamilton for your inspiration, encouragement, listening ears, and for being the best examples in my life. Lastly, to every friend, sorority sister, colleague, or stranger that has had a kind word to say, a word of encouragement, or who sent positive vibes my way throughout the course of this labor of love, I thank you. May all your dreams come true and you never feel the need to apologize for living your best life and being your Simply Successful Self!

PROSPERING PERSONALLY

1

INTRODUCTION

Define success on your own terms, achieve it by your own rules, and build a life you're proud to live.

- Anne Sweeney

Ever had someone tell you what you can't do? Well, I am from East Saint Louis, Illinois and it is a huge misconception that nothing good comes from East Saint Louis. Many people don't expect greatness from my hometown. But I am a living example that great things and great people are born and raised where I am from. Against all odds and societal opinions, they spread their wings beyond those 89 blocks and do some pretty amazing things. No matter what cards you were dealt or where you are from, I want you to know that you can, and you will be as successful as you want to be. Those things from your past don't determine who you currently are, your level of success, or who you are ultimately destined to be. Many times, your past can make you feel like you are fighting an uphill battle; believe me, I know that feeling all too well. There have been times in my life where I have felt like I was at a disadvantage that some of my colleagues, classmates, and friends just didn't seem to have. But that did not stop me from achieving my goals and working harder to prove that I too belonged in the same schools, classes, and rooms as anyone else did. You are not alone here; like me, you too are in control of your own success. Your success is tied to your hard work, dedication, ambition, and yes sometimes blood, sweat, and many, many, many tears. You have to press on through adversity and you have to make sure that you do not allow anyone to infiltrate your spirit with their negativity. You can and you will do great things regardless of if they think so or not! You can and will live the life you've always envisioned! Speak greatness over your life! Affirm that you can and will do whatever you set your mind to do. As long as you do the work to achieve it, success is within your reach!

Over the years, I have thought about what it means to be successful. What does success really look like? What does being successful feel like? How does your level of success make others feel about you? Since I graduated from college and became a functioning member of society, my quest for success has been one of those things that drives me. I've been planning the steps that I needed to take in order to become successful most of my adult life. I'm going to venture to say that most people have at least thought about being successful once or twice during their lifetime. Your situation may be different from my own, but I assure you that no one sat me down and explained what success was or gave me the roadmap or blueprint on how I should go about achieving it. I've concluded that success is relative.

You can ask 10 different people what success is, and they are likely to give you 10 different answers.

I discovered a fascinating article titled *"12 Rich, Powerful People Share Their Surprising Definitions of Success,"* published in Business Insider. The article consisted of definitions of success from billionaires, founders, and legendary investors, all giving their different definitions of what success meant to them. What I found to be the most interesting was that not one of those rich, successful people measured success monetarily. Their definitions all varied but to sum it up, they equated success to happiness, satisfaction, relationships above all else, enjoying your work, making an impact, constant growth, working hard all the time, and the ability to change people's lives (Lebowitz, 2017). Although there were 12 different definitions of success, none of them centered on money. Actually, some people specifically stated that success was not monetary. Let's keep it real, the article provided definitions from the former President Barrack Obama, Warren Buffet, Bill Gates, and none of the 12 successful people giving their opinions on what success means to them were struggling financially. I would venture to say that a person's definition of success can change depending on where they are in life, their circumstances, financial situations, and maybe even whether or not they have a family that they are responsible to provide for. I have unmarried friends who believe that success is being married and having children. Others say that success is measured by how much money they have in their bank accounts. Success for me involves a combination of things which include having a loving support system of family and friends, being centered spiritually, accomplishing professional goals I've set for myself, as well as being able to financially provide for all of my needs and most of my wants.

The conundrum is that success for many is a moving target. Are you ever really successful based on your definition or is it something that seems unattainable? Is success something that you will always be striving to achieve? These are some of the questions I had to ask myself. By nature, I am super critical and I tend to be a bit of a perfectionist. If you are into astrology, you may say it's the Virgo in me. I had to grow to a point in my life where I had to stop, reflect, and become grateful for where I am in my life at this very moment. I am content but do not mistake my content-ness with being complacent. I still have goals to achieve but at 37 years old, I can proudly say that I am successful. To all of you doubting your success or trying to find ways to become successful, continue reading and allow me to guide you to a place of great growth and heightened confidence on your way to becoming more of your Simply Successful Self!

Ok so here's how it all started… I'm a small-town girl with big-city dreams. If you're not familiar with or have never heard of East Saint Louis, Illinois then let me paint a picture. It is definitely a small town; the population in 2014 was a mere 26,731. The majority, 95.4% of the population in 2014 and for as long as I can remember was African American, and the poverty rate in 2014 was higher than the national poverty rate (DATAUSA, 2014). My hometown can be classified as an underprivileged neighborhood or at risk as they would oftentimes refer to it during my formative years. Many of the media outlets and residents alike placed more emphasis on sports and athletics than on education. I was fortunate because there were two groups of students that seemed to get the most attention from our counselors and teachers when I was in High School. Those groups were the really "smart" kids and the athletes. I have to be honest, while I was in school, I never realized the disparities in how other students who didn't fall into one or both of those categories viewed their preparation for higher education. It wasn't until my 10-year class reunion that this was brought to my attention. I was having a conversation with one of my classmates who pointed out that unlike us honor students, they weren't asked to participate in college tours that allowed students to travel around to different colleges and universities to learn about what each school could offer prospective students. They were not a part of school-sponsored trips to visit schools to find out what the requirements were to attend or the resources available for them to fund their college educations. They were not presented the opportunities that allowed students to spend summers studying at universities like I had every year dating back to middle school. It was common for those in honors and those student-athletes to have college prep which included learning about and practicing for college entrance exams such as the SAT and ACT. Unfortunately, not all students were afforded those opportunities, and honestly, maybe it was available to them but they were not always made aware of all the resources available. Naively, I assumed these things were available to everyone because I participated in them all. See, I was what some would call one of the "smart" kids. I graduated number three in my high school graduating class of more than 400 students. I was involved in and held office in multiple scholastic and extracurricular organizations. I also ran track for a couple of years and was a co-captain of the varsity cheerleading team because I was well aware that in order to get into college you had to do these things. You had to show that you were a well-rounded student who was involved in extracurricular activities as well as excel in the classroom. I even took four years of the same foreign language in high school because I was informed that I wouldn't have to take it in college as long as I had earned four years of credits leaving high school. This is information that not everyone in my graduating class was necessarily privy to unless they sought it out or asked the right questions to the right people. Teachers and counselors were more likely to mention these sorts of things to certain students within the student body.

I was accepted into my first-choice college, the University of Illinois at Urbana-Champaign (UIUC), and I even started classes the summer before my freshman year with the Young Scholars Program at the University. I excelled in math and science throughout school and I decided to double major in a five-year Agricultural Engineering and Agricultural Sciences Bachelor's degree program. Let me let you in on something very few people know…I struggled, and it was extremely difficult! It wasn't tough because I was incapable of learning what was being taught; I struggled because unlike my classmates, I hadn't been exposed to many of the engineering software programs like AutoCAD (Computer Aided Drafting) or MATLAB (Matrix Laboratory) software environments for engineers and scientists in high school. We didn't have classes that taught us the basics of these programs like some of my fellow classmates at UIUC. In college, I was expected to have experience in working with those systems before stepping foot into my first introduction to engineering course. I had to work twice as hard as my classmates to teach myself the basics just to stay afloat and not fall behind the rest of the class. I am a person who never wants to give up or fail; so, I stuck it out for three years. By my junior year, I was so worn out and completely over it all. I just wanted to graduate and get on with my life. I decided to talk to the head of my department and academic counselor to see what I could change my major to that would allow me to graduate ASAP! Going into college, I'd been told that engineers made great money and I was good at math and science, so that would be a good fit. I was encouraged to pursue a degree in engineering for those reasons. It wasn't all bad; I did enjoy a few of the classes I took. However, I just never really saw myself as an engineer. Thinking back on it, my vision of what I wanted for my career always consisted of me wearing designer business suits, carrying a briefcase, and having a corner office on one of the top floors in a skyscraper with an amazing view. ***Spoiler Alert*** In my current career, I do work in a nice office on the top level of an eight-story building, with an amazing view of the Detroit Skyline, and while the dress code is more business casual that business professional, I still get my fashion fix by letting my inner fashionista out from time to time. The more I think about it, being an Agricultural Engineer may have never fit with that vision. I'm sure there are some working in that field in office settings that are living out my vision but they are more than likely the minority in that career field. I never had a chance to explore what I wanted to do in life because I declared a major before starting college and the only electives to choose from were in some way related to the major I had selected. I was very strategic in making sure that my general education required classes also doubled for a requirement within my majors.

The College of Agriculture, Consumer, and Environmental Sciences had established a new degree program in my current department of Agricultural Engineering (AGE) called Technical Systems Management (TSM), and many of the Agricultural Engineering classes I had previously taken, gave me credit for the TSM courses because a lot of the classes were the same. The good thing about that major was that I could specialize in marketing, management, and mechanization. I was able to explore business through those courses and it was a much better fit. I graduated with a Bachelor of Science degree in Technical Systems Management in a total of four and a half years (that was fine by me since I'd originally signed up for a five-year degree program.) I was just getting started. I went on to complete a Master of Science degree in Agribusiness from Alabama Agricultural and Mechanical University (AAMU) two years later, and I have since completed a Master of Business Administration from Lawrence Technological University. Sometimes it takes a while to find your sweet spot, but once you do, there is no turning back! Now it is my desire to help all of you to secure the level of success that you've always envisioned for your life. I've learned that success is not one dimensional, it order to reach that pinnacle of success you have too strive to become successful in each and every area of your life. There are three parts of this book that will aide you in developing, strengthening, and maintaining areas in your life to prosper personally, professionally, and some areas to prosper both personally and professionally.

2

SIMPLY SELF

Nourishing yourself in a way that helps you blossom in the direction you want to go is attainable, and you are worth the effort.

- Deborah Day

This section is all about you. Yes, YOU! How often do you really take the time to focus on you? Often, I find myself focusing on everything and everyone else. Did I remember to send that email? Am I going to make that suspense date for this project I'm working on? Let me check on my friend who is going through a recent breakup. While all of those things are important, sometimes you have to unplug from it all and spend a little time focusing solely on you. In order to be at your best, your mind, body, soul, and finances need to be in order. I know you are probably thinking now, where did finances come into the picture? Well, I'll be perfectly honest with you, nothing gives me more anxiety than having to worry about my finances. I sleep very well at night knowing that all of my bills are paid on time and are not incurring any late fees. I am overjoyed when each payment towards student loans, mortgage, and credit cards brings me one step closer to financial freedom. With that being said, yes, finances definitely belong in the mix. Because not having your finances in order can elevate your stress levels, and I am a witness that stress can throw everything out of whack.

SELF-CARE ASSESSMENT

Self-care is vital to living your best life and to be whom you are destined to be. Take a moment and reflect on the areas of your life that affect your whole self and that could potentially be hindering you from reaching the ultimate level of success you envision.

1. Are you practicing self-care regularly? How often?

____

____

____

____

____

____

2. What are some of the things you do or can do to practice self-care?

____

____

____

____

____

3. Identify the things that prevent you from practicing self-care?

____

____

____

____

____

4. How can you eliminate the things that are preventing you from regular self-care?

____

____

____

____

____

5. Plan out times and days that you can routinely incorporate self-care into your days, weeks, or months.

____

____

____

____

____

Digital Download of the ***Simpli Self-Care Assessment*** available at:

https://stacihuddleston.com/secure-success-guides/

3

SIMPLY MIND

Taking care of yourself is the most powerful way to begin to take care of others.

- Bryant McGill

The first part of self-care that we will focus on is taking care of your mind. In order to be successful in life, you have to be mentally present, checked in, and ready for any and everything life has in store for you. That includes the good, bad, and the ugly. Self-care is vital to living your best life and to be whom you are destined to be. This is something you have to be cognizant of all the time. Ambitious people overextend themselves by going above and beyond for other people, employers, family, and friends all the time. The problem is not in the act of doing for others but it becomes problematic when you have overextended yourself so much that you are mentally exhausted and not functioning at your full capacity. I have personally been here time and time again. Over the last few years, I have had to actually stop to sit back and take it all in. I had to recognize when enough was enough.

In the professional arena, from my experience, I've noticed that those who do the best work are also assigned the most work. Is it fair? NO! But does it happen, ABSOLUTELY! This is the racehorse and donkey scenario. A colleague I met in a leadership class a couple of years ago explained this concept to me. The racehorses are eager to learn and ready to go. They are frequently overworked while the donkey sits idly by not being tasked to take on any additional responsibilities above their normal workloads. That is only if the donkey is capable of completing their normal workloads because oftentimes, they cannot handle additional tasks and they even struggle with completing their assigned work. Subsequently, the racehorses also complete the donkey's work that they did not get around to finish. I've always been a racehorse, and my advice to you is don't be the darn donkey! No one likes or respects the donkey. If you are in a leadership role then do identify your racehorses and donkeys but don't force the racehorses to burnout. Hold the donkeys accountable and stay on top of them to do their share of the workload or write them up. This is not about you being a jerk; it is really their choice to fall in line or to deal with the consequences. If there are deficiencies, then address those areas by getting them the help to fix them. Then hold them accountable after the deficiencies have been addressed. Many people prefer low confrontation so they go with the path of least resistance by piling onto the racehorses the additional work, which they accept without complaints. As a leader, it is your job not to do what makes your life easier but to do what is best for the people you lead!

I had a friend who was being taken for granted. She was doing all the work only to not receive any recognition for her actions in her current position. She was growing more and more frustrated. While the responsibility was her boss' to acknowledge her contributions and to raise morale with her and any other employees, this was not the time for my friend to stop working hard or to compromise her work ethic. If you find yourself in a similar situation, remember that it's important that you grind harder now so it can pay off later. You need to continue to work harder because you have something to prove. Doing this will separate you from the others when it is time to choose the next leaders down the road. Sometimes, you have to focus on where you are going and where you want to be and not dwell on your current situation. If you strive for more, then remember your current situation is just temporary. Also, to prevent creating bad blood in your current situation, keep working hard enough to get out and keep in mind the things you will do differently once you are the one in charge.

In my personal life, I pride myself on being a good listener. I've found that while that is a really good trait to have; those who are good listeners always get called when things are wrong in the lives of their friends and family. I have no problem being a listening ear, however, if I don't take a break for myself every now and again, I can't be the best listener I can be. Those who always say yes always get asked. That was also me. The keyword there is "was," as in past tense. That is no longer me. Allow me to let you in on one of the best-kept secrets that I didn't find out about until I was in my thirties: it's ok to say NO! You don't have to please everyone. They may get upset but then they will move past it and if they don't, then good riddance. Hello, my name is Staci and I am a recovering People Pleaser. Occasionally, there are times when I almost fall back into my old ways not wanting to hurt anyone or let them down. When I realize that doing whatever is being asked of me will be at my expense, then the NO is not so hard to deliver. Take a moment to evaluate what is being asked of you and if you are mentally up for that task. If you are up for it, then, by all means, go for it and help out. If you are not mentally up for it, then remember NO is always an option.

When you are mentally exhausted or not present in your everyday life, then you need to take time to clear your mind and get in a good headspace. Some of the signs that you need to practice some mental self-care are when:

- You are always exhausted.
- Your days are starting to run together.
- You are becoming forgetful.
- You can't remember the last time you did something you love doing (reading a good book, enjoying a movie, having a spa day, etc.).
- You have been in a bit of a funk; you're not your normal self (unusually short-tempered, easily annoyed, overly pessimistic, etc.).

This list could go on and on. But you know what it's like when you just don't feel like yourself. Whatever that feeling is, that's exactly what I am talking about. You need to be in a headspace to flourish and not to just function. Some of the things you can do to get in a better headspace would be unplugging from everything for a while. I set my iPhone to do not disturb every night at the same time prior to going to bed so that I can spend alone time, thinking, praying, reading, or whatever I want to do without any distractions.

It is very much okay to take a break from toxic people who drain you or those who always talk about what is going wrong and never anything going well. I've had to do it before and I will continue to do it to keep my sanity. This does not make you a bad person; it is your responsibility to protect your peace of mind. Another thing you could try is to interject some positivity into your interactions with pessimistic people and maybe that will help turn the conversation in a different direction. Good vibes only, right?

Ever seen the television drama *"Being Mary Jane?"* Well, the lead actress in that show uses Post-It notes with quotes all around her home. I also have a friend who has scriptures and positive affirmations placed strategically in her home, car, and I'm sure, at her job. They are posted in places she is sure to see them on a daily basis multiple times a day. This is a great way to reinforce and train your mind to think positively. My friend has one that I absolutely love. It reads, "You are the woman someone is praying for!" How about placing a Post-It note on the inside of your car visor that reads, you are beautiful? You would see it every time you pull the visor down to block the sun or go to look into the mirror.

It doesn't matter who you are, everyone faces stressors. What makes all the differences is in how you deal with those stressors when they present themselves. According to All Healthcare, "If you don't take time to unwind, constant stress can lead to a number of physical and psychological problems, like poor concentration, depression, back pain and weight gain. It also weakens your immune system and increases your risk for cancer and cardiovascular disease" (Kim, N. & Price, G., n.d.). In the famous one-liner of one Internet sensation, Kimberly "Sweet Brown" Wilkins, "Ain't nobody got time for that!"

Think about some things you can do to clear your mind and do them. Here are some things to get you started:

- Meditation.
- Go for a walk, take in the scenery, and get some fresh air.
- Delete negative people from your life and your social media feeds.
- Watch a funny movie.
- Read an interesting book.
- Start journaling (this has gotten me through some very tough times).

- Make a list of things you are grateful for.
- Unplug from your phone, technology, and social media all together (this doesn't have to be forever but do take some breaks).
- Do something from your childhood. You know things that made you happy and carefree as a child – be it swinging, biking, or tree climbing. As a child I loved to color and guess what, I still have coloring books and the 64 pack of crayons to go with it. They even have many coloring books for adults on the market to relieve stress and provide a calming effect.
- Laugh. Sounds simple, right? Well, a lot of times stressful situations don't bring about laughter, so you may need to seek it out. Grab a drink with your funniest friend, rent your favorite comedian's latest stand-up comedy DVD, stream it on Netflix, or check out the newest comedies in theaters.
- Visit a Shooting Range. Apparently, there is something relaxing about locking, loading, and letting it rip! I must admit that my first experience at a shooting range was quite exciting and relaxing all at the same time.

- Organizing your space. Be it at home or work, clutter can add to your stress levels. I know that from personal experience the act of cleaning-up or picking up around the house relaxes me. The less cluttered my space becomes, the less stressed I feel.
- Say a prayer for peace. Many would-be sleepless nights have been calmed by offering up a prayer for a peaceful night's sleep. I have a mind that will be going for hours and hours after I've gotten into bed, thinking about any and everything. So, if you are a spiritual person, take a page out of my book and pray or read the bible until you fall asleep.

I'm sure there are a number of other ways to de-stress but these are some of the ones that have helped me out from time to time. Life is too short to be stressed all the time, so please for the sake of your health, your sanity, and the sanity of those around you, find a moment to relieve some of the stress that you may be dealing with! I know it's an ongoing cycle but you'll be a lot happier if you do. Do what works best for you.

SIMPLY DO:

- **Do take time to make sure your mental health is in order.**
- **Do cut out toxic people who give you mental angst.**
- **Do take moments for yourself.**

Digital Download of the ***Simpli Mind 30 Day Self-Care Challenge*** available at:

https://stacihuddleston.com/secure-success-guides/

MIND SELF-CARE MONTHLY CHECKLIST

Over the next month, try to check as many of these each week as you can:

Mind Self-Care Task	Week 1	Week 2	Week 3	Week 4
Schedule in five minutes of non-directed activity several times throughout your day.				
Meditate				
Declutter, your workspace, living space, car, etc.				
Unplug for an hour. Leave your phone, smartwatch, etc. in a different room.				

Mind Self-Care Task	Week 1	Week 2	Week 3	Week 4
Mute, unfollow, or block toxic people showing up in your social media feeds				
List the great things people say about you and file them together to read later				
Mark off a task on your To-Do list that has been on it way too long				
Do at least one thing today just because it makes you happy				

TABLE 1: MONTHLY MIND SELF-CARE CHECKLIST ADAPTED FROM (NATIONAL ALLIANCE ON MENTAL ILLNESS, N.D.)

4

SIMPLY BODY

Take care of your body. It's the only place you have to live.

- Jim Rohn

When it comes to taking care of my body, this is an area I truly have a love-hate relationship with. I can't be alone! There have been times in my life when I would hit the gym six times a week and drink green smoothies once or even twice a day. Then there are times when I want a burger, junk food, and possibly not move at all for days. I often joke that the day I turned 30 years old, my metabolism gave up on me. I can remember doing approximately two miles walking or running for two consecutive weeks straight prior to turning 30 and my body would transform and my clothes would fit a lot better. Post-30, I barely notice changes after months of consistent workouts, and if I'm 100% honest, my motivation just isn't what it used to be. With that being said, I cannot be truly successful in my life if my physical self is not what it needs to be or what I envision it to be. "Why is that?" you might ask. Well, it's really simple. You are more confident when you feel and look good. When your physical self is at its best, there is an undeniable pep in your step. Personally, I'm politer, I smile more, and I engage in more conversations when I feel like I'm looking good. If you don't know what I'm talking about, then try this. Actually, think about how you'll dress for work tomorrow or the next day you have to go into the office. Lay out your clothes the night before. Don't just pick any old thing, pick something you really like to wear, maybe something you've received a compliment wearing. If you always wear flat shoes, try on a pair of heels, and if you rarely make time to apply makeup, spend a little time on your ten-minute face (a little bronzer or foundation, mascara, a hint of blush or a highlighter and a lip gloss or lipstick). I'll tell you exactly what will happen. You will be present, more confident and people will be unconsciously drawn to you. This is the key to being noticed, recognized, and being presented the opportunity to show them what you have to offer in meetings. Perhaps someone who normally doesn't will ask you for your opinion. Hey, I've seen it happen. Humor me and see for yourself.

It has always been my motto to dress for the job I wanted and not the job I currently have. As an intern, I dressed like a BOSS! Blazers, heels, and a very nice leather work bag were my staple pieces. If I wanted to be in a leadership position or become an executive, I couldn't be walking around in khakis like some of my colleagues at the time. People seem to respect people who care about themselves and their appearance. When you are healthy and feeling your best, you exude confidence.

Your health is important not only to you but to those who care about you. Your family and friends, your spouse and children would all love for you to live a long happy healthy life. Therefore, you need to stay on top of your health! You need to schedule your annual wellness exams, get the proper screenings, and if you are not going to take the time to make a complete lifestyle change to control or cure whatever ails you, then take your prescribed medication just as the doctor prescribed it. Do not let preventable things get in the way of the life you envisioned for yourself or the success you are on the path to achieve. It would be unfortunate if you missed out on what life has to offer you because you were too stubborn to seek out a doctor or to take care of yourself. Don't let this be your downfall or the demise of such a promising life. I understand that there are times when you do all you can and something unexpected gets in your way. You have to deal with those things as they come but still be proactive and aggressive when they do arise.

EAT RIGHT

> *"The food you eat can be either the safest and most powerful form of medicine or the slowest form of poison." — Ann Wigmore*

You have to eat right. A lot of people believe that living a healthy lifestyle is directly related to how skinny or small you are. However, this could not be further from the truth! There are small people who are starving themselves and not getting the proper nutrients their bodies need to be the best they can be. Eating right can mean different things to different people but the bottom line is for you to be conscious of the foods you are eating and how they are affecting your health. If you have high blood pressure, then please cutback on your daily salt intake. If you have high cholesterol, cutback on foods high in saturated fats such as red meat, sausages, hard cheese, lard, pastry, cakes, and cream. Different illnesses have been attributed to what you eat and how it is prepared. I love fried foods as much as the next person but I've decided to only partake every once in a while, and when I'm cooking, I am mostly baking instead of frying. Small changes can lead to better health overall. You do not have to sacrifice taste or deliciousness for health. Just find new ways of making something healthier. Research recipes and try them out. Experiment with spices for flavor and you may just like how you've prepared it more than the unhealthy way. I'm not a proponent of giving up all meat, or living by seafood and vegetables alone because I know that there are benefits in everything and if you are not supplementing with the correct vitamins, you could very well be deficient in some of the nutrients your body needs to be healthy. Everyone's body is different and what may be good for someone else may not work for you. This is not about losing weight or anything like that, it's just about being in the best physical health that you can be in. It's best to consult your doctor before making any drastic changes in this area such as going vegan or becoming a vegetarian. I know they can assist with making it a better transition overall. Anyone who has ever tried to eat healthy for any length of time has probably realized that it can be quite pricey! Here are a few tips that can help you eat healthy on a budget:

PLAN YOUR MEALS

That's right! Instead of going to the grocery store and just picking up items, have a plan of the meals you will be preparing for the week and the ingredients you'll need to complete them. Planning your meals is a great way for you to avoid bad food choices. When you haven't planned ahead, you can easily succumb to snacking on non-healthy alternatives. If you are tech-savvy, there are a variety of apps for planning meals and grocery shopping. Search your app stores and fid what works best for you and your family. Currently my goto app for planning my meals is Paprika 3.

STICK TO THE LIST

The easiest way to spend more money than you planned on spending is by going to the grocery store while you are hungry. This is a surefire way to purchase any and everything that you think you want or may want to eat! If you have to eat something before going shopping, by all means, just do that. The best way to stay in your grocery budget is to stay focused on what's on your list; get it and get out!

SHOP AROUND

As with anything, when you want to get the best deal, you should shop around. Weekly grocery ads will give you the stores with the best prices for the items you are looking for. A big mistake I made was going to a health food store (Whole Foods, Trader Joe's, Nino Salvaggio's, Randazzo, etc.) to get everything on my grocery list. I then realized 100 dollars later that I barely had enough in my shopping bags to make one complete meal. If you are on a budget, this is definitely not the way to go! I spent double what I would have at the regular grocery store. Now, I'm not saying that you shouldn't patronize the healthy stores because they are awesome and they do have some good quality items, fresh produce, specialty finds, etc. What I am saying is that you should be selective in the items that you decide to purchase from them if you are on a budget. If you can't get it anywhere else, or if their produce is the freshest then, by all means, splurge a little on those items. But if there is a better deal or coupon for it somewhere else, then shop there instead. A lot of the chain grocery stores (Kroger, Meijer, Target, etc.) have mobile apps that allow you to clip coupons on your phone. These are just a few things that have helped me along the way. I hope it can be helpful to you as well (Produce for Better Health Foundation, n.d.).

EXERCISE

> ***"Those who think they have no time for exercise will sooner or later have to find time for illness." — Edward Stanley***

Most times when someone mentions physical health, the number one thing that comes to mind is exercising. I do believe that daily movement and exercise are beneficial to your overall health. So, yes, I am an advocate of it. Women's Health Magazine gives great examples of health benefits that can be credited with doing specified amounts of exercise on a weekly basis.

See Table 2 below:

Exercise (Minutes Per Week)	Health Benefits
30 minutes	Reduces risk of type 2 diabetes
150 minutes	Reduces risk of cancer
175 minutes	May Help alleviate symptoms of depression
450 minutes	Significantly reduces risk of premature death
120 minutes	Offers Improvement in memory
90 minutes	May reduce blood pressure levels

TABLE 2: AMOUNT OF EXERCISE AND THE BENEFITS ADAPTED FROM (DOMONELL, 2016)

Some people want to exercise for weight loss as well as the health benefits listed above. If you are trying to lose weight and not just maintain your current weight, then you need to burn more calories than you take in. It sounds simple but burning more calories than you eat can be challenging. You would be surprised how much exercise you would need to burn off that Twix you had for lunch. Sometimes it is just better to pass on the junk food. If not, you'll be paying for it in the gym later. If you want to be successful at your fitness and weight loss goals then consulting with a nutritionist and personal trainer can be just what you need. They take the guesswork out of it. Nothing is more annoying than believing that you are eating healthy and working out frequently for months and months without the numbers on the scale budging one bit. The benefits of a nutritionist and personal trainer is that they can tailor a plan for you, one that will target your trouble areas and tone up the rest. For years, I would only do cardio, never lifting any weights in the gym because I was under the impression that lifting heavy weights made women start to bulk up and look masculine. After getting a personal trainer and lifting and squatting with heavyweights, I noticed my body transform and start to become lean. It is a myth that all you need is cardio to lose weight or to tone up. Lifting helps you burn more calories and even allows your body to keep burning calories after you are done with your workouts. I decided to join the 30-Day Transformation Team with Kathy Drayton and Luther Freeman and it was well worth it. When I started the program on February 9th, 2016, I weighed 148.4

pounds. and my waist was measuring 35 inches. 30 days later, I was weighing 137.2 pounds. and my waist was 32 in., 11.2 pounds. down and 3 inches off my waist. It may not sound like a lot to you but let me tell you, I was in the best shape of my life! I was following a meal plan and workout regime that consisted of cardio twice a day in the morning and in the evening combined with regular workouts and strength training. I was toned and my clothes fit better. It's not always about the numbers on the scale; but about how you feel, how your clothes fit, and how you look to you. If you want to start a fitness journey, then I recommend you document every step of the way, and the best way to do that is by taking before, during, and after photos. They will allow you to see a change and build confidence which is key when it comes to fulfilling your ultimate goals of personal and professional success. Getting into shape and taking care of your health will check the block in that area and put you one step closer to being successful in every area of your life.

If you cannot afford a personal trainer or you don't really have time to go to the gym, do not fret. I'll share some of the inexpensive ways I've used to get and stay in shape over the years. You don't have to have an expensive gym membership to get your workout on. I can use the gym in my condominium clubhouse 7 days a week; it is equipped with treadmills, two elliptical machines, a stationary bike, and free weights. If you want to cut back on spending and you have access to an at-home facility, then, by all means, get rid of the gym membership and save that money or put the extra towards paying down debt. Another way to work out and save money is by doing so in the great outdoors. When the weather is nice, I run outside free of charge and use free workout apps on my iPhone to track my workouts. There are a variety of apps that are awesome for tracking. I've used Runtastic, Map My Run, and the Nike + Run Club apps; they allow you to play music, track calories burned, distance, and more. There are many free apps out there. Just search for fitness apps on the app store of your smartphone and find the ones that work best for you. Surprisingly, another inexpensive way to get some fitness motivation is by following people on social media (Instagram, Facebook, Pinterest, etc.) who are living a healthy lifestyle or even by searching hashtags like #fitness, #fit, and #fitnessmotivation. These hashtags allow you to pull up pictures and videos of different workouts or fitness challenges (squats, abs, etc.) that you can do in the comfort of your own home! One home workout I found on Instagram a few years ago that I loved is called the 100 Workout. You can do this work out in the privacy of your own home, office, or hotel room while you are traveling, and the best part is that you don't need any equipment. Stay happy, healthy and give it a try.

THE 100 WORKOUT

100 Jumping Jacks
90 Crunches
80 Squats
70 Leg Lifts
60Jumping Jacks
50 Crunches
40 Squats
30 Leg Lifts
20 Jumping Jacks
Run for 10 minutes
-Unknown

CHECK-UPS AND DOCTOR VISITS

> *"The aim of medicine is to prevent disease and prolong life, the ideal of medicine is to eliminate the need of a physician." - William J. Mayo*

Three years ago, in 2017, I had a health scare that could have prevented me from being my best-self down the road. In the early part of 2017, I notice a lump in my right breast. I honestly should have gotten it checked out much earlier but I decided to keep an eye on it to see if it would go away since I had been previously diagnosed with having fibroadenoma, a common benign or non-cancerous breast tumor, probably when I was 17 years old. Back then the doctor thought that the best course of action was to have it removed and so I had some fibroadenoma tumors or cysts removed from my left breast. I can't remember if the procedure started out as a biopsy and they removed the cysts and sent them to pathology prior to them determining that they were benign. The procedure was outpatient surgery and my parents were by my side. To this day, that is one of the events of my life I can only vaguely recall. However, the scar, which is probably only slightly noticeable at best, is a constant reminder of my first serious health scare.

Several years ago, somewhere in my late twenties during another self-breast examination, I noticed another lump. This time, it was in my right breast. I was sent to have an ultrasound to have it checked out. To make a long story slightly shorter, the diagnosis was the same as before. However, due to the advances in medicine or technology, the radiologist determined that the best course of action this time would be to leave it be since sometimes these things would go away on their own and if not, they were not detrimental if left alone.

By 2017, I mentioned the lump that had yet to go away to my doctor during my annual well-woman visit sometime in July. She performed a breast examination and thought that it was probably the same thing that I'd previously had. However, for my peace of mind she sent me for an ultrasound. At this point, it was all pretty routine to me and didn't cause too much alarm. I went on to schedule my ultrasound and the hospital she'd referred me to told me that it was their protocol that at my age of 34, just a month shy of my thirty-fifth birthday, I'd also have to get a mammogram. Now, this is when "ish" got real and my level of concern went up a notch. I was always told that if breast cancer didn't run in your immediate family, then there was no need to even have your first mammogram until you were 40 years old and I was five years away from that. But every conversation I had with medical professionals for the next couple of months always included that "at your age" comment. That really started to irritate my entire SOUL! It was probably all in my mind, but it sounded a whole lot like, "because you are getting up there in age," and that didn't sit well with me. The phrase definitely held a negative connotation for me. All I could think was I know I'm around the corner from 35 but I AM NOT OLD! The fact that I had just barely avoided a minor anxiety attack being anxious about turning 35 that year added fuel to a simmering fire within me. I scheduled the mammogram and it was every bit as uncomfortable as I had been warned it would be…but worse. I won't torture you with the details.

My lovely mother told me that years ago mammograms were worse and that they have gotten better over the years. I can't even imagine how! That just seems unbearable, so I'll take a moment to Thank God that I didn't have to put up with the mammogram machines of the past. AMEN! It was a warm day near the end of July, and I was sitting in a cold doctor's office. It wasn't the kind of cold that causes you to shiver but the coldness was that of a sterile place with no warmth even in the décor; whites and beige were the colors of choice. It was nerve-wracking but I had a "God Send" – a person from my past who I hadn't seen or spoken to in years reappeared just when I needed them most. By some divine intervention, our paths had recently crossed via social media and in an effort to catch up, my long-lost friend texted that day as soon as I arrived for my first ever mammogram appointment. We texted back and forth the entire time I was in the waiting area. Unbeknownst to him, I was waiting to experience a rite of passage to mature womanhood and he was able to calm my nerves and help me to focus on something other than the anticipation of the impending torture that I was about to endure. An experience far too personal to share with someone I didn't really know at that stage of my life. The text conversation was a mix of past and future travel, and adventures to foreign countries and faraway lands. It was just what I needed at that moment. So, if you ever read this, thank you for your timing and thank you for that day!

Once I had completed the mammogram portion, I had to wait for the results. It probably took about a week or so for the doctor to call me into schedule an appointment for us to discuss them. She let me know that her recommendation was to have both breasts biopsied because the radiologist had found areas of concern in both. I believe she said there were two areas of concern in both my right and two in my left breasts. It was the beginning of August and I had a thirty-fifth birthday trip planned to Cuba at the end of the month and although I wanted to put off scheduling the biopsy procedure, I went the week before my birthday. The results were to be ready on the same day that my flight left for Cuba. Therefore, I was not able to get my results until after I returned. I didn't want any bad news to ruin my birthday plans and festivities so I decided to schedule the appointment to hear my results for the week after I came back from my trip.

The more time that passed since I'd felt the lump, I realized that God was providing me with the peace I needed to make it through. I was optimistic and faithful that God would let the outcome be a good one regardless of what the doctor had to say. I would have loved for her to tell me that it was nothing over the phone but being that she wanted me to come in, I knew that it would probably be something a little more serious. I prayed about it and also got my prayer warriors to intercede on my behalf. My prayer warriors are friends and family who love God and pray often. They can speak positivity and speak life over anything and anyone. I went on to celebrate a wonderful milestone (at least to me) birthday smack dab in the middle of my thirties in Cuba – the big Three-Five.

I'll be honest, sitting in the doctor's office the last week of August waiting for her to come in to give me the news that would determine my fate was more than a tad uncomfortable. She informed me that of the areas of interest those in the left breast were the same fibroadenoma that I'd previously had and that she would not take them out. The radiologist had also found a papillary legion (papilloma) in my right breast, the area that I was originally concerned about, and that it was also benign. However, if left in, it could turn into cancer. Her recommendation was for an outpatient surgery where I'd be put to sleep and she would remove it. The outcome was great! Initially, I was relieved and thankful to God for the non-cancer diagnosis, but I was hoping there would not have to be a surgery at all. I was only a fool for a moment, as those thoughts were me being ungrateful. I had to get myself together real quick! I am forever grateful to God for my life and for the positive news I received in the doctor's office that day. Preventative surgery is way better than any other kind.

My surgery was scheduled for the second week of October and my parents came to be by my side and to help me recover. My friends, family, coworkers, and my parent's church family prayed, came to the hospital for the procedure, sent flowers and checked in on me. These are the things that I will forever cherish. One-week post-surgery, with a clearance from the surgeon, I knew that I was just as successful as I've ever wanted to be. I am successful in that I am loved by so many people. Had I gone through all of that alone and with no-one showing that they cared, I would have had to reevaluate what success meant to me.

Two years later, I had a complete déjà vu moment. During my annual well-woman exam in July of 2019, I notified my physician that I felt a new lump in my right breast. After another ultrasound and mammogram, I was notified that another papilloma had formed and needed to be surgically removed sooner than later. I wasted no time and had the surgery a month later and although I'd done this all before, I was still amazed and grateful for the loving support and prayers of my family and friends during that time. I am successful as a daughter, a friend, and a colleague because if I wasn't successful in building relationships, nurturing relationships, and being present in those relationships, the outcome would have been different. I could have been in that cold hospital both times all alone and never heard a kind word or relieved voice once it was all said and done. I will continue to strive to be at my best health and to be the best I can be in every area of my life because if I hold up my end of the bargain, great things will continue to happen in my life.

Your health is important. Don't skip checkups! Don't ignore signs that something might be wrong! Don't let your lack of concern for you and your wellbeing hinder you from being successful in every area of your life. The moral of the story is that if I had ignored the warning signs and put off going to the doctor and waited years to get it checked out, it could have grown into cancer. Let this be a lesson to you. Stay ahead, catch things early, and you will have a fighting chance to overcome every obstacle. Doctors say it all the time. If we are diagnosed early, the survival rate and options are greater. Don't let anything prevent you from getting out ahead of or in front of your future success. Take the necessary steps to get you there because it is not worth your future being cut short because of something you could have prevented. At this moment, I pray that the Lord blesses you with good health! If by chance your health is not the best, I pray that you are able to fight like a warrior to beat whatever diagnosis and that once you beat it, you are able to tell your story to inspire people all over the world that they can beat it too!

Living a healthy lifestyle and taking care of your physical self isn't something that evolves from doing nothing. But living a healthy lifestyle comes from making a conscious decision to make informed healthy choices not only for today but also for the future.

SIMPLY DO:

- **Do visit the doctor no matter how much it scares you.**
- **Do your best to eat most of the things that are good for you, but Do indulge in the things you love to eat from time to time.**
- **Do make time for some exercise to keep your heart happy.**

Digital Download of the ***Simpli Body 30 Day Self-Care Challenge*** available at:

https://stacihuddleston.com/secure-success-guides/

BODY SELF - CARE MONTHLY CHECKLIST

Over the next month, try to check as many of these each week as you can:

Body Self-Care Task	Week 1	Week 2	Week 3	Week 4
Take a power nap... 20-30 mins to rejuvenate you				
Have a Spa Day... massage, manicure, pedicure, etc.				
Be conscientious of what you eat... make healthier choices				
Take a yoga class				
Go for a walk, run, exercise				

Body Self-Care Task	Week 1	Week 2	Week 3	Week 4
Breathe…Take extended breaths and just focus on breathing…it's a blessing				
Take a luxuriating bath…add moisturizing bath bombs…light a eucalyptus candle to relieve stress				
Have a good laugh				

TABLE 3: MONTHLY BODY SELF-CARE CHECKLIST ADAPTED FROM (NATIONAL ALLIANCE ON MENTAL ILLNESS, N.D.)

5

SIMPLY SOUL

The world rewards you for what is in your mind, the universe rewards you for what is in your heart, and the Heavens reward you for what is in your soul.

- Unknown

Don't forget about your spiritual wellness. Whether you need to align your chakras, practice yoga, sage your residence, or go to church to get your spiritual mind in order, then It Is TIME and It Is IMPORTANT! I am a Christian and I have no problem letting people know that I love the Lord. Casting all my cares on him and trying very hard not to continue to worry about them has truly been working in my favor. I know the Holy Bible says not to worry at all after you have turned it over to God in prayer, but I'm a work in progress, so I haven't exactly mastered that just yet. Either way I'm sure you get my drift. I believe that Jesus is the son of God and that he died for my sins and yours. I also believe that he can and will do all things according to the plan that he has for my life and yours. I also believe that when I die, I will go to heaven and be reunited with all of my loved ones who have passed away and made their transition before me. I'd like for everyone in the world to go to heaven, however, the way the good book is written it doesn't look like that will be the case. I also know that there are many religions and religious beliefs; some similar to my own and some that differ quite a bit.

I took a religion class when I was an undergraduate student and I was such a strong believer in my faith that I received a barely passing grade in that class because I wouldn't conform to whatever they were teaching in the course. It was the principle, and if I had to do it all over again, I'd do it exactly the same. I remember a classmate asking why I wouldn't just write what the professor wanted me to write. That classmate asked me what if my beliefs were wrong, and my answer then is the same as it is today; whether my religious beliefs are wrong or right, I believe them to be true and if it so happens that they aren't, then I've lived a better life on this earth because I believed in a higher power. My beliefs would have caused me slightly less stress and an unexplainable sense of peace during my time here on earth. I am a huge proponent of peace leading to success. Peace allows a person to actually focus on other things aside from their worries. I try to recharge my spiritual self by attending my church service weekly on Sundays and sometimes by attending bible study during the week. I also enjoy the weekly prayer calls once a week that I can listen to while I get ready for work in the morning. Do whatever works best for you. What brings you peace, joy, and gives you hope? Whatever that is, that's what you should incorporate more of into your life.

There have been periods of my life when I have not focused enough attention on my soul and spiritual self and there have been other times when it has been one of my main concerns. Getting closer to God and to trying to discern his purpose for my life has helped me in other areas of my life. I will touch on passion, purpose, and prosperity in another chapter, but these three things can increase your success across the board. They are avenues to get you where you are trying to go. Who knew I may just be onto something, utilizing my life lessons to encourage someone else to strive to live their best life on purpose! When I'm focused on God, he definitely directs my path. There are examples of times in my life when I put all of my faith in God and he led me to places that have helped me to grow by leaps and bounds that I want to share with you.

The first major time that I can recall I experienced God working in my life on my behalf was the last semester of my undergraduate college career. I graduated in 2004, December to be exact. I didn't necessarily know what it was that I was going to do after college. I had applied to a few jobs and had even gone on a couple of interviews. Although I didn't really know what it was I wanted to do after college, I was never drawn to return home. I hadn't applied to any graduate schools or even taken any graduate school entrance exams. I had a sales job offer with a Fortune 500 company in Chicago, IL not making very much money compared to the cost of living, and the compensation was heavily commission-based. Meaning that the money I received would majorly be based on what I sold. I knew one thing; I could not survive in Chicago on that. All I could think was that I would always be stressed out trying to make sales quotas and worrying about if they would let me go for not making the cut. For me personally, I knew that was not the way to go. I had asked around and the feedback I received from people who had accepted positions with that company or in the sales field didn't give me much peace of mind. I was busy finishing up my studies, joining a sorority and I just hadn't taken the time to set up anything concrete post-graduation. I prayed about it because truth be told, I probably would have taken that job but God knew that wasn't a good look for me and he dropped something much better into my lap.

My first cousin, Nikky, was working on her Master's in Urban Planning at Alabama A&M University (AMMU) at the time. I talked to her and she inquired about my next steps. Most of the details of that conversation escape me, but she was convinced that since I was graduating from the University of Illinois in an agricultural field that I should be able to go to graduate school at Alabama A & M University as well. The Department of Agribusiness was down the hall from her department and she got to work on asking all the necessary questions and getting me into graduate school the month following my graduation. My other cousin, Kimberly, had also graduated recently and somehow Nikky spoke so highly of the two of us that one of the Professors, Dr. Befecadu, affectionately known as Dr. B told her that we could go to Graduate School at AMMU, major in Agribusiness and to move to Normal, AL. Imagine my shock because I had not even applied to that school or any other schools for graduate school admission; nor had I been accepted. For some reason, it just felt right. I knew that God was telling me to go. I graduated from UIUC on December 18, 2004, and I started my first day of class as a graduate student at AMMU on January 5, 2005, a mere 18 days later.

When I arrived on campus, the first thing I did was meet Dr. B; he got right to work to get me conditionally accepted pending me taking the Graduate Record Examination (GRE). He also offered me a Graduate Research Assistantship under him which qualified me for in-state tuition and a monthly stipend in a matter of days! When God shows up, let me tell you, he shows out! My cousin Kimberly also got conditionally accepted into the same department and was also offered a Graduate Assistantship. We were able to get an on-campus apartment, and two years and four months later in May of 2007, all three of us – Nikky, Kimberly, and I – graduated together with Master of Science Degrees from AMMU. During our time in graduate school, Nikky and I lost our maternal grandmother, Betty, and her sister Marian, who was Kimberly's maternal grandmother while we were pursuing our graduate degrees. Our grandmothers were not able to physically be present but I know that they were sure enough there in spirit beaming with pride! God kept us through those insurmountable deaths and through the completion of each of our master's programs. I am a witness that when you trust and follow God, he will ultimately provide!

It was the summer of 2008, and I was just over a year into my Research Associate position with AAMU University. This is another example of God's plan for my life falling right into place. Following my completion of my Master's degree, Dr. B, my mentor and the Professor responsible for me even getting into graduate school, worked it out that I was offered a job upon graduation that allowed me to continue to work at AAMU teaching undergraduate-level courses in the Department of Agribusiness and continuing my research and writing scholarly articles expounding on my Master's thesis. All of my former professors, that had become my colleagues, wanted me to take the next step and go on to pursue a Doctor of Philosophy (PhD) in Agricultural Economics. I had gone straight through undergraduate and graduate school without taking any time off, so I decided that I needed a break from school. I really needed some real-world experience and I knew that if I decided not to pursue a PhD that I would not progress to the extent that I would have wanted if I remained in the arena of academia without that degree.

AAMU was having a career fair and as an alumnus, I was invited to participate. Although I currently enjoyed what I was doing, I knew that the only way I would grow professionally in academia would be to go back to school and I was not feeling that decision at the time. My resume was submitted and I was told that I had been selected to interview with the Department of Defense for a Cost Price Analyst position. The interview questions were pretty generic entry level so I had no idea that I was actually applying for a job as an Inventory Management Specialist. I guess it was God's divine intervention because I ended up interviewing for the wrong job and guess what...I got it! I was offered a job as an Inventory Management Specialist intern in Michigan of all places. I later spoke to a few people who had gone on the actual interview for the Cost Price Analyst positions and no one had heard anything back and I'm not sure if they even filled those positions. God knew exactly what he was doing and which job I needed at the time. I had never been to Michigan nor did I have any family or friends who lived in Michigan. I prayed about my decision to move and although I had the support of my family and some of my friends, there were others who didn't want me to leave Alabama or them. I understood that their feelings weren't any indication of them not wanting what was best for me but it was human nature to not fully embrace change. I'd prayed about my decision and I knew that God was leading me to pursue new adventures in a new place and that this was the road I needed to take in order to do that. I moved to Michigan 12 years ago and I have not regretted my decision. Initially, I took a decrease in my annual salary of approximately 7,000 dollars. I also had to finance the move from Alabama to Michigan out of pocket which set me back quite a bit financially. My faith and trust in God have led me to many places that I never thought I'd go; they turned out to be the best decisions for me and they have helped mold me into the successful woman I am today. Six promotions and a roughly 80,000 dollars increase in my annual salary are all benefits I've received from trusting God's plan for my life. I clearly attribute my success to God, in the words of Mary Mary the international Gospel Recording artists, "It's the God in Me!"

Not everyone's spiritual beliefs are the same but please find out what centers you, makes you a better person, and what allows your soul to be happy. It is one of the keys to your success. Healthy living incorporates the mind, body, and soul, so be sure to take care of all three!

Digital Download of the ***Simpli Soul 30 Day Self-Care Challenge*** available at:

https://stacihuddleston.com/secure-success-guides/

SOUL SELF- CARE MONTHLY CHECKLIST

Over the next month, try to check as many of these each week as you can:

Soul Self-Care Task	Week 1	Week 2	Week 3	Week 4
Help someone else				
Volunteer				
Write your thoughts				
Give someone positive feedback				

Soul Self-Care Task	Week 1	Week 2	Week 3	Week 4
Read or listen to something inspirational or uplifting				
Hang out with someone who radiates enthusiasm and positivity				
Take time to set up a phone call or date with your best friend… catch up, reminisce, enjoy the bonding time				
Take a day to do the things you enjoy alone				

TABLE 4: MONTHLY SOUL SELF-CARE CHECKLIST ADAPTED FROM (NATIONAL ALLIANCE ON MENTAL ILLNESS, N.D.)

6

SIMPLY FINANCIAL

Financial peace isn't the acquisition of stuff. It's learning to live on less than you make, so you can give money back and have money to invest. You can't win until you do this.

-Dave Ramsey

Have you taken the time to assess your financial health? This is a no-judgment zone. Do not subscribe to the school of thought that if you don't see it, then it doesn't exist. What I will tell you is that once you know better, you do better! The truth is that having a good financial posture puts you in a better position to be successful. Having your finances in order can positively affect other areas of your life. Let's start with your health. Stressing over money can lead to sleepless nights, among other things that can negatively impact your health such as heart disease, diabetes, high blood pressure, and obesity. Taking care of your finances can alleviate some unwanted stressors, and once you have the money thing figured out or at least have a plan in place to fix your financial problems, then you are more relaxed. You will worry and stress a lot less once your finances are together. We talked about taking care of your physical self in order to be healthier and eating right is a part of that. When you are in a good financial situation, you can afford to purchase healthier foods that are good for you. It is no secret that the stuff that is horrible for our bodies tends to be less expensive than the healthier options. Another part of self-care that we touched on was taking care of your mind.

When money isn't one of your worries, you can treat yourself more often. Having regular pamper-me days and relaxing activities help you relieve stress. Planning spa days and even taking vacations to get away from all of your stressors is ideal when you can afford it. Less stress is good for both your mental and physical health. You have more peace when you aren't constantly worrying about money, bills, debt, etc. Once you are well on your way to financial freedom, you will feel more secure and confident because you will know that you are making smart decisions and saving for the future and your retirement. You'll be able to see the light at the end of the tunnel that stands between where you currently are and where you'll be once you are, in essence, financially free. Oh, what it would be like to no longer owe anyone; and if you do owe someone, you are liquid enough in your finances to pay for it in cash if you so desire. All of these things have the possibility to lead to better health and healthier lifestyles.

Happiness is another area of your life that can be impacted positively or negatively depending on your financial situation. Being in a positive financial position can add to your overall happiness and the happiness of your family. It's simple; when you are in a good place financially, you are able to do more of the things that make you happy. You can live the lifestyle you want in freedom. You can travel, buy those shoes, splurge on that purse, and spend more on entertainment and dining out guilt-free when you are in a good financial position.

When your mind is focused and not thinking about financial issues, you are more productive in all areas of your life. Who knew that stressing over your finances could negatively affect your productivity? Having to worry about your finances distracts you from other things that you need to accomplish. Being preoccupied can negatively affect your work and productivity. You may find yourself doing the same task over and over or staying on the same task far too long because you keep losing your train of thought. All as a result of you being concerned about how you are going to pay for this or that. It is my recommendation to you that you figure it out, plan, and work the plan to avoid this from becoming your normal way of living.

Many marriages and relationships suffer and sometimes end when couples frequently fight about money. According to the article, "These Are the Reasons Most Couples Fight", "one of the most common catalysts for arguments in a relationship is the management (or mismanagement) of finances (Blatchford, 2016)." When your financial house is in order, then you argue less about things related to money and have a financially stress-free home. You also have time to spend with friends and loved ones. You are able to have fun experiencing what life has to offer because you are in a place where you can afford to do those things; and also, because you don't have to spend all of your time working a second job or trying to make ends meet by working longer hours.

Unlike some of my college friends, I didn't get caught up in the credit card game or bogged down by credit card debt during my undergraduate days. My mom forewarned me about not signing up for them. However, I did get one as a way to have some credit history to be able to purchase my first cell phone. Back then, my parents made it clear that I could only get a cell phone when I could pay for it myself. That credit card was used for emergencies and I never missed any payments even when I was only paying the minimum balance. Fast Forward eight years after I'd completed graduate school and began working. My first adult job was fulfilling and I really enjoyed it. I was working in academia, teaching undergraduate courses and conducting research in my field. Although I loved what I did, I knew that in order to make the money in academia that I'd envisioned making, I would have had to go back to school to pursue a doctorate. The truth is that while I was making a decent salary for a 26-year-old, I knew that I would have to do more in order to continue moving up and making more money throughout the course of my career. I decided to pursue other avenues and ended up accepting a job across the country in Michigan.

When I first moved to Michigan 12 years ago along with a pay cut, I incurred moving expenses from moving roughly 650 miles from Alabama. To help me with the expenses, I applied for my second credit card because I had maxed out the first one I got my freshman year of college covering other moving expenses. The cost of living was higher and my savings dwindled fast. Hindsight is definitely 20/20. If I could do it all over, I would have sold everything and got new things once I could afford them in Michigan. The problem was that I was very sentimental and attached to my furniture. After finishing graduate school, I was offered my first "adult' job. I moved into an unfurnished apartment and my parents helped me furnish my place by splitting the cost of it with me as a graduation gift. My advice to anyone just starting like I was, would be to sell everything and buy new stuff when you get to where you are going. You don't have to do it all at once but over time you can get the pieces you need to survive and to make you comfortable. I'll be honest though, having a fully furnished place with all of my familiar things is probably what made my adjustment to Michigan a little better but by no means was it worth the financial hole I'd begun digging for myself.

None of my friends lived locally so I was still traveling all over the United States for friend's birthdays, homecoming at my Alma Mater, and whatever events someone wanted me to attend. Remember I'm a recovering people-pleaser. Looking back on it, I should have told everyone NO! I should not have let my pride, fear of missing out (FOMO), or the fact that I didn't want to disappoint them stop me from being honest with myself and with them. Honestly, I had fun on each and every trip and was lonely and missing my friends and family every single day, so those getaways did help me to keep my sanity but also broke the bank. You cannot do everything that everyone wants you to do on your road to success. My trying to please everyone led to major anxiety and unnecessary debt. I have lived and I have learned. The lesson I think everyone should take away from my experience is if you can't afford it then don't do it!

This was the first major roadblock I faced after making a fresh start in an unfamiliar place. I had done well by making it out of college without falling into the abyss of credit card debt. I even got a job after completing graduate school and I was making a decent salary in a city with a relatively low cost of living prior to the move to Michigan. I was able to travel on a whim, and I could actually afford to do it back then. Things changed and I was swamped in credit card debt that I could only pay the minimum balances on a monthly basis. Prior to this, I was pretty good with my finances. I received an allowance every two weeks from my mom and stepdad to cover necessities and my dad sent me money monthly to cover what I needed all through my undergraduate years. In my last couple of years in college, my Dad would send me a lump sum every semester and I would manage my money never really having to ask either of my parents for additional funds unless it was an absolute emergency.

Not only was this credit card debt new to me, but I also had started paying back student loans that had come due for both my bachelor and master's education. Since I went directly from undergrad to graduate school, my student loans were still in a hold pattern and then there was a six-month grace period that took place following the completion of my graduate degree. The kicker, as I have mentioned before, was that my salary was not what it had been before. It was time for me to evaluate my finances and explore different avenues to pay down my debt. I ended up taking a pretty unconventional way to finally pay off my credit cards in the end. I volunteered to deploy to Afghanistan as a civilian and the overtime, holiday pay, and danger pay on top of my annual salary allowed me to not only pay off all of my immediate credit card debt; but it also allowed me to save some money for a down payment on my condominium and to build an emergency fund. This option may sound extreme and may not be available to most people but sometimes you have to think outside of the box and find alternate income streams or increase your income where you can.

Maybe it's been a while since you have checked your financial health, but there is no time like the present. Your financial health determines your wealth! This is how you do it – find out how much you owe and categorize it by who you owe, balances, interest rates, and identify what type of debt it is. Do not completely ignore your student loan debt. In a sense, it's considered good debt because it shows that you have a degree to potentially earn a good income and it doesn't necessarily reflect negatively when you are going out for loans on automobiles or when purchasing a home as long as you are not delinquent on payments or you don't have a history of late payments. If you have a large amount of student loan debt, then look into ways to pay this off. There are various student loan forgiveness programs for those working in the public sector, such as law enforcement, teachers working a set amount of time in underprivileged neighborhoods, former Peace Corp members, nurses servicing underprivileged patients, etc. Please do your research where this is concerned and do it early on so that you know all the rules and have a goal that you are working towards. This was another lesson learned.

Upon completing my first master's degree in 2007, I was encouraged to consolidate my student loans because they would give me a better interest rate overall and that I could pay one bill per month for federal loans and a separate bill for my private loans. I did this and all of my federal loans were consolidated through the American

Education Services. It seemed all good at the time. Fast forward to 2015 when I heard about the Public Service Loan Forgiveness Program that allowed for the forgiveness of the remaining balance of your Federal Direct Loans after you made 120 qualifying monthly payments while working full time for a qualifying employer. I had made multiple student loan payments over the years and none of them counted even though I was a federal government employee because I did not consolidate with Direct Loans specifically. This is extremely unfortunate and this is an example of why it is imperative that you take the time to do your own research when it comes to your finances. I was told that I would have to reconsolidate my loans with Direct Loans and that none of my previous payments would count towards the 120 payments. I did the math and by the time I re-consolidated and paid all 120 payments, there would have been nothing left to forgive.

One thing you never want to do is default on your student loans. There are options you can take if you can't make the required monthly payments. Two things in particular that you may be able to take advantage of are forbearances and also deferments. A deferment and forbearance will give you permission to temporarily stop making payments or to temporarily reduce your monthly payment amount for a specified time. If you do not qualify for either of those, then you should reach out to your lender and try to negotiate a reasonable amount that you can pay monthly. If you are having an economic hardship and you just cannot pay anything, the lender can grant you a forbearance anywhere from a few months up to a year. If you lose your job, have a child, or become ill for an extended time, then most lenders will try to work with you until you can pay. If you don't reach out to them to form some type of an arrangement, then you can be sure that they most certainly will report you to collections. Arranging to pay less will prevent your lenders from reporting your account as delinquent. This will prevent a negative entry from showing up on your credit report if you get out in front of it; do not wait until you've missed several payments. The first bills I got from my student loan lenders were combined for nearly $1000. I discussed it with my mom and she told me to give them a call and ask what could be done. I told them that there was no way that I could afford to pay that and they asked me what I could pay. I'm sure I gave them a low-ball answer and we met at a more reasonable number somewhere in the middle. All I wanted to do was to avoid becoming delinquent on any of my loans and have it negatively affect my credit.

With the deferment, your loans will go into a deferment status while you are enrolled at least part-time in a post-secondary school. There may be more instances that can qualify you for deferments but you will need to research your situation for specifics. Please do your research to see where you fit and if you are eligible. You will still accrue interest during these periods but they give you a break from having to make high monthly payments if you cannot afford them. In the early years of my internship, I applied for the Student Loan Repayment Program offered by my employer and I received it two different years. My employer paid 10,000 dollars each year directly to my student loan lenders. I had to sign a Continued Service Agreement promising to continue to work for my employer for three years after receiving the money but in my case that was well worth it. Another thing I took advantage of was to enroll in a Master of Business Administration (MBA) program since my employer paid for the tuition and books. During that time, I was able to defer my student loans while I was enrolled in school. I earned a second graduate-level degree at my employer's expense and no cost to me. See what your employer offers, you might be surprised; my employer stated that they do not pay for degrees but they do pay for business courses that will be beneficial to current positions. So, if they pay for enough classes, eventually you would have earned a degree for free! If I knew then what I know now, I would have tried to apply for a job that paid for advanced degrees right after completing my bachelor's degree. I would have saved myself and an additional 40,000 dollars plus interest in student loan debt. If you have that option, I highly recommend going this route. I have received a total of 20,000 dollars from my employers towards paying off my student loans and they can give up to a total of 60,000 dollars during your career. Of course, none of this money is just given; you have to apply, compete, and be selected to receive the money each year. Best believe I will faithfully apply every year until this is no longer being offered or all of my student loans are paid off, whichever comes first. What's the worst that can happen? I don't get it? Well, at least I tried. If I don't apply, I certainly won't get it and if I do apply there is a chance that I will.

Next up for me was my immediate debt, my credit cards. I was up to approximately 11,000 dollars in credit card debt form my cross country move and initial lower salary. I was staying above water by paying at least the minimum balances every month. But I realized that going at that rate my credit cards would not be paid off anytime soon. The job I had taken in Michigan as an intern started out paying less than I was making with my previous employer by maybe 6 or 7 thousand dollars, however, I would get a guaranteed promotion and raise of approximately 10,000 dollars each year for three consecutive years. When I evaluated this move, I knew that the reward would far outweigh the sacrifice. In just one year, I was making more than I had at my previous job. While my salary increased by about 10,000 dollars each of those three years, I maintained the same quality of life and my expenses remained the same over those three years. I did not move to a better apartment even though I desperately wanted to. I did not buy a new car during those years even though my friends and fellow interns around me were doing just that. I decided to sacrifice so that I could actually see my raise and use it to pay debt down faster. Finally, after I completed my intern program, I had an accumulative total of 30,000 dollars increase in my annual salary. That's when I finally made a move into a better apartment, but not one that would break the bank.

Those small sacrifices put a dent into my credit card debt but there was also that drastic thing I mentioned before about going to Afghanistan with my job for six months that helped me eliminate the remainder of my credit card debt. My job involved me supporting the soldiers from afar. The opportunity presented itself for me to work alongside the brave men and women I support on a daily basis in Afghanistan back in 2013. I knew that it would be beneficial to my career as well as to my pockets due to the nature of the assignment. During my six-month tour, I was able to pay all of my credit card balances down to a zero balance and save up enough money to put a down payment on my condominium.

You don't have to do anything quite as drastic, but if you are serious about getting out of the hamster wheel of debt, then you have to find other streams of income. A few examples would be to start a business or consultant firm doing something you love on the side. Getting a part-time job could be another source of income. I have friends who assisted with helping people update their resumes for a nominal fee and others who applied to teach courses at a community college a couple of nights a week since they had their master's degrees in specific fields. A lot of people want nothing to do with working in retail but if it brings in another check and allows you to pay more towards your debt monthly to help you eliminate your debt, then it is so worth it!

It has been 12 years since I started this journey and moved to Michigan. I was still driving the same 2008 car that I purchased to withstand the Michigan winters the year I was hired until January of 2019. It was paid off and over eleven years old. I had been promoted a total of six times and my annual salary has increased by approximately 80,000 dollars since I started in 2008. That is far more than I could have ever imagined. It was one of the best decisions I've ever made and I would not change one thing about trusting, believing, and following God's plan for my life.

Your road to financial freedom and wealth may differ from my road but I want to see you be successful in your finances. Take the time to assess what you owe and find the plan that works for you. Set a goal and make a roadmap to get you there. I have all the faith in you. If you are willing and ready, then I know you can do it!

Once you have taken a good look at your finances and you now know exactly what you owe, get a plan in place. Make a list of what you owe, what the minimum payments are, and interest rates of each. If you don't already have a budget, create one with what your income is and what you are spending every month. We will get into budgeting specifics later on. See where you have extra money or where you can cutback in your current spending to pay more towards your outstanding debt. For example, if you spend five dollars per day five days a week on Starbucks then maybe you can cut that out and put the extra 100 dollars per month towards paying down your debt. Sometimes when you cannot figure this out on your own, finding a financial consultant could be beneficial. I've assisted several people with setting financial goals, budgeting, saving, and increasing their income to meet their goals.

The two ways to pay down debt that I will mention here are the snowball method and the avalanche method. Honestly, it's up to you and what you feel comfortable with, or if you want to do some combination, then that works too. With both methods, you focus on one of your credit cards or loans by putting all extra funds towards getting one paid off at a time while you continue to pay the minimum balances on any other cards or loans that you owe. Another similarity of the two methods is that once the focused debt is paid off, you add the amount that you were paying monthly on that to the next debt you focus on to pay it off. This cycle continues until all of your debt is paid in full.

The true difference between the two is that with the snowball method your focus is on the card or loan with the lowest balance regardless of what the interest rate is on that one. Then you keep going from there, by focusing on the next lowest balance once your previous focus is paid off. Many like this method because they get small victories every time they pay off another card or loan and since the focus is always on the one with the smallest balance this happens more frequently than if they opted for the avalanche method. With the avalanche method, the focus is always on the card or loan with the highest interest rate. Then you keep going from there, by focusing on the next highest interest rate once your previous focus is paid off. With the avalanche method, you end up paying less in interest overall because you are not continuing to rack up interest on the higher interest debt during the duration because you are paying it off quicker. It sounds nice to end up paying less overall and to some this hands-down sounds like the best way to go but it really is a personal preference.

If your highest interest rate is also your loan or card with the highest balance, it will take much longer for you to get that victory of paying something off. Some people need small victories to keep them motivated and to help them to feel like the sacrifices they are making to pay down their debt is really worth it.

I actually did a combination; I started with the smallest amount to get started then started going after those with the highest interest rates. Do what works for you but if you have the willpower to keep paying the extra on the highest interest rates and be okay not seeing the smaller victories then do that because you will end up paying less over time. However, do what works for you because you have to start somewhere. Your financial success depends on it.

BUDGETING

> ***"You must gain control over your money or the lack of it will forever control you." - Dave Ramsey***

Over the years I've become very conscientious about where my money is actually going. A lot of times you don't realize where it all goes. In an effort to track my spending, I've become somewhat obsessed with budgeting. So much so that I have created budgets and budgeting tools for not only myself but also for my family and friends. Budgeting not only enables you to see exactly where your money is going but it also allows you to identify the areas where you could possibly cut back to start saving or just be able to save more. Some simple steps to monthly budgeting are listed below:

- **Step 1:** What's coming in? List all of your income that you receive on a monthly basis. From your employer, child support, investments, side hustles, etc.
- **Step 2:** What's going out? Identify and list all of your monthly expenses. Start with the most important and work your way down to the least important expenses.
- **Step 3:** Compare your total income to your total expenses. Your total expenses should not exceed your monthly income. The goal is for your total expenses to be less than your total income. If this is not the case,

then you are definitely overextended and not living within your means.

Your monthly income should cover all of your monthly expenses and allow for saving, investing, retirement, and building an emergency fund. If your income does not cover all of those, then you need to find out where you can cut back on some of your expenses. If that doesn't do it, then you need to find additional streams of income.

Your budget should include your fixed expenses, those that do not change from month to month. Examples of some of your fixed expenses would be things such as your mortgage, rent, car note, etc. The cost of these things will stay the same each month. Other types of expenses in your budget are your variable expenses; these can change from month to month based on a variety of factors. Your utility bills would be an example of a variable expense because the amounts of your bill vary each month depending on your usage. When determining your most important expenses, think about your needs, things that you cannot live or survive without. They can be a combination of fixed and variable expenses. Then there are those things that are not considered necessities; those are flexible expenses. Flexible expenses are important because these are expenses that can be adjusted or completely dispensed; for example, your luxury goods.

Your budget should always leave a little wiggle room for those unexpected expenses that you don't plan for that come out of nowhere. Such as, having to pay to replace a flat tire or pay for a speeding ticket you didn't plan on getting. After all your expenses are paid, you should have some residual income to take care of your unexpected expenses unless you have savings or an emergency fund that can be tapped into. When creating your monthly budget, you should overestimate your expected expenses. This way, you'll likely end up with leftover funds, that can go right into your savings accounts.

> ***"A budget is telling your money where to go, instead of wondering where it***

A lot of people see budgeting as being too restrictive; but being disciplined about your spending habits allows you to have more control over your money. If you are contemplating making an expensive purchase, you can incorporate saving for that purchase months before you plan to buy it with budgeting. Then once you have the money saved up, you can make your planned purchase guilt-free. I make sure to add birthday gifts and Christmas shopping into my budget so that I can make sure that I have money set aside for those things that I know are going to come around each year. The great thing about Christmas and the birthdays of your friends and family members is that they are the same date each and every year. There is no surprise, therefore, you should be able to put away money in advance for them. You can take time to build them into your yearly budget upfront as a way to be less stressed, or not to go further into debt once the Christmas season actually arrives. The budget I currently use is set up in a 12-month budget format. It allows me to see the entire year as well as the individual months. It lets me see how changing certain things in a particular month will affect the following months. It allows me to adjust future months to keep me on track with both my savings and goals to pay down debt. Every month is different, very few will be exactly the same. Something as simple as the price of gas changing from month to month can make you spend more on gas during any given month. I try to take those things into consideration when determining my projected spending on gas each month so that I can stay right at or slightly under my projection on a month to month basis. That is the goal; for your actual spending on any category to be right at or under what you are projected to spend each month. Routine car maintenance is another thing that can cause your budget to differ from month to month, every 3000 – 6000 miles driven on your car might have you paying for an oil change and possibly a tire rotation. Other months you would not be expecting this expense. Plan for it all, don't let these things catch you off guard.

Budgeting only works if you are disciplined and you stick to the budgets you create. If you have trouble doing this, you may want to find a person you trust to help hold you accountable. As a financial coach, I assist people in setting goals, sticking to their budgets, and paying down debt. I also help them with their goals of saving for big purchases, life-changing events, and rainy days. It is my job as a financial coach to encourage and make sure my clients are doing the work. This normally takes place via scheduled check-ins throughout the duration of our time working together. If you are married, then it is imperative that you and your partner are a part of the budgeting process, otherwise, it will not work. When one party is not aware or isn't involved, it could sabotage the entire process. Sometimes couples can even use an outside accountability partner or financial coach to assist them with achieving their joint goals.

Starting your budget can sound daunting but don't let it overwhelm you. I personally start by paying God then myself, right off the top. I'm a Christian so I believe in tithing a tenth and then saving at least a tenth for myself. That is 10 percent of my income being given to my church and 10 percent of my income going into my savings account every time I get paid which in my case is every two weeks. I like that my church allows for online one-time or recurring payments because I like to automate all of my bills. Tithes and savings are things I payout on a recurring basis so I like having the option of scheduling them. Most banks and credit unions will allow you to set up an automatic transfer of funds to your savings account. Once those two things are taken care of, the remaining funds go to those expenses that are recurring and necessities to include food, shelter, utilities, basic clothing and transportation. Once the necessities are out of the way, you can complete the rest of the categories in your budget. You start with the most important things first then go from there. Addressing those important things first can help you to pinpoint your wants versus your needs and find areas that you can cutback on. You may also identify areas that you can get rid of altogether.

When I first started budgeting, it was a tool to help me pay down debt. If you have debt – be it credit cards, student loans, or even automobile loans – then your main goal should be to try to pay that debt down as quickly as possible because every debt you pay off increases the amount of money you have to do, buy, and save more! It's time to take a stand and stop letting debt be your reason for not doing the things you love or that you want to do. You work hard for the income you earn, and from time to time, within reason, you should be able to enjoy the fruits of your labor. Get to where you want to be financially so that you can live, love, and explore to your heart's content!

In order to accomplish financial freedom, there will probably be areas where you must sacrifice some of the things that you are consistently spending money on that are not necessities. Once I got everything for my budget into an excel spreadsheet, I saw that I was paying way too much on cable every month. So, I cut it out! My cable bill had become too expensive and I was never watching premium television or any shows in real-time. I would always catch them the next day or a week down the road. I decided to subscribe to some of the streaming services like Netflix and Hulu. By cutting cable out and focusing strictly on an internet service for streaming, my monthly bill went down by approximately 60 dollars a month. That was about 720 dollars a year that could be saved or put towards paying down my debt faster. I chose to put that money towards paying down debt. I haven't had cable in at least five years and I am in no rush to go back to it. You can pay off debt or save money quicker if you find areas to trim your spending. Some ways you can cut out or scale back some of your flexible non-necessity expenses could be canceling your cable, dining out less, shopping at discount clothing and grocery stores, or even by going to the nail and hair salons less often. Learning to do your manicures and pedicures or even your own hair at home could save you hundreds of dollars a month. Maybe start treating yourself to those luxuries every couple of months or once a month or just for special occasions instead of those weekly and biweekly visits many of us are guilty of, myself included.

Remember that your budget cuts are only temporary. You can always adjust later down the road once you have met your savings goals or paid down the debt that was hanging over your head. It is no fun being restricted in your spending but sometimes you have to be uncomfortable for a specified time to get to a place where you can live a very comfortable life where you don't have to worry about your spending habits at all! Do you want to get to a place of being financially secure where you have more disposable income and little to no debt? Do you want to have an emergency fund built and also have money in your savings and retirement accounts? Isn't that what we all ultimately want? The freedom to do as we please with the money we earn. Honestly paying off debt is like getting a raise because you are no longer paying those creditors every month.

A good way to get into the habit of budgeting is to put everything money related to a schedule. While there are some whose income varies and isn't paid on a set schedule, a lot of people are paid repeatedly. I take that time every two weeks on payday to pay all of my bills that are not automated, and to transfer money from my checking account to my savings account. I also make a habit of adjusting my budget during that time as well. Budgeting has been incorporated into my biweekly routine. Schedule times when you revisit and revise your budget and also set-up automatic drafts for all of your recurring bills that offer that as an option. By doing this, you'll know the exact date each month when that money will come out of your account and you can avoid missing payments or incurring any additional fees on late payments. There are also perks sometimes associated with setting up payments by automated draft for your accounts. Sometimes you pay less than you would if they were counting on you to remember to pay them every month. It's like they reward you for setting it up in advance. Knowing what to expect and when to expect it can alleviate a lot of stress and potential financial pitfalls down the road.

There are numerous websites and mobile applications that provide valuable resources when it comes to personal finance. I've been using Mint.com for years and not only does it keep track of your personal finances it also reminds you when you are exceeding your budget and when a bill is due. It provides comprehensive personal finance management, from budgeting to setting and monitoring goals. The site automatically tracks banks, credit cards, investment accounts, and loans. This one is by far my favorite because it analyses your spending habits and recommends ways to save you money. According to an article in PC Magazine Online, "Mint.com remains PCMag's top pick among personal finance services, because it's useful every day" (Duffy, 2018).

> ***"Don't tell me what you value, show me your budget, and I'll tell you what you value." - Joe Biden***

Here are some things that can help you get started:

- You need to be able to distinguish between your needs vs. your wants. I NEED food but I WANT food from Ruth Chris Steakhouse.
- You have to be willing to sacrifice some of your wants in order for your budget to be effective.
- Last, but certainly not least, you have to be disciplined when it comes to budgeting.

SIMPLY DO:

- Do create a buffer in your budget for those unexpected expenses.
- Do try taking out enough cash for your entertainment and possibly even meals and try not to overspend. Once it's gone for the month, then you'll have to wait to eat out and do fun stuff that costs until the following month.
- Do track your spending via a spreadsheet, online banking, or online budgeting tools.
- Do focus on you and don't worry about keeping up with the Jones'. Try not to compare what you are doing to anyone else.
- Do have goals and know what your why is... it helps to keep you on track.
- Do keep at it. Over time you'll get better at it. I promise.

SAVING

> ***"The habit of saving is itself an education; it fosters every virtue, teaches self-denial, cultivates the sense of order, trains to forethought, and so broadens the mind." - T.T. Munger***

Saving is very important when it comes to your financial health and your overall success. God forbid something happens and now you can no longer count on your current income streams for a few months. Can you continue to cover all of your expenses? Did you see an amazing handbag or pair of shoes that just "Gave You Life" the moment you laid eyes on them? Were they a bit pricey? Well that is the story of my life; there is always a fabulous accessory that I feel that I can't live without but I also don't want to break the bank. The aforementioned scenario is a perfect reason to save! You can save up for your purchases and buy luxuries and have splurges guilt-free! "How is it guilt-free," you might ask. Well, when I purchase an item without the credit card debt and interest incurred, it is guilt-free with no buyer's remorse. Paying with cash brings you a great deal of satisfaction. Free to live life and enjoy your purchase without wondering when you are going to finish paying for it because it is already paid it full! The same goes for a nice vacation or buying a new car or house. Life-changing events such as having a baby could also be a very good reason to have some money saved.

Hey, I'm on an all-out mission to rid myself of all debt (credit cards, student loans, and mortgage). By keeping a close eye on my budget and by not depriving myself of some of life's luxuries, I will succeed! Your story and goals may be different from my own but what I want for you and me is for us to live this life the best we can, given the resources we have, and by being fiscally responsible while doing so! It's how we will be successful in this life.

A good goal to have would be to calculate what three to six months of your expenses would be and save that amount to build an emergency fund. If something went wrong and you lost your job, or weren't able to work for an extended period of time like during the COVID-19 pandemic and lockdown of 2020, would you be able to keep living like you currently do? Would your bills continue to be paid on time? This is why having an emergency fund is so very important. Say it takes you a couple of months to find a new job and a steady income, with an emergency fund you could essentially survive on what you have saved up for a few rainy days.

Something less drastic would be having your car break down and you needing a couple thousands of dollars to fix it. If you have accumulated some savings, you can use that and replenish it later instead of having to figure out how you are going to pay to have it fixed. Not having a mode of transportation is very inconvenient and can cause additional stress to you and others that are helping you out. Once you've saved enough for those situations, you can start saving for specific things like a vacation, a car, a wedding, etc.

SIMPLY DO:

- **Do save for a rainy day. Create an emergency fund by saving at least three to six months' worth of living expenses in case unexpected costs arise.**
- **Do save for big purchases. Set financial goals to keep you on track. Know exactly how much you want to save and how long it will take to get there. The clearer the saving goal, the easier it is to track your progress.**
- **Do automate your savings. Have it come directly from your check automatically on a consistent basis.**
- **Do pay yourself first. Determine a set amount of money to put away every month and treat it like any other bill. Aim to save at least 10 to 12 percent of every paycheck into your savings and retirement accounts.**

- **Do save wisely. Choose the right savings methods to match your goals.**
- **Do your research to find the best interest rates for your accounts. Be it for retirement or your child's education, find the best method to save.**

CREDIT

> *"Too many people spend money they haven't earned, to buy things they don't want, to impress people that they don't like." — Will Rogers*

The ability to get credit can be a wonderful thing. Misusing credit can be detrimental to your credit score and your overall success in life. In high school, I knew a couple of people who had cell phones, but my parents didn't buy me one. My stepdad would always say that I could have one when I could pay for it myself. My, how the times have changed. My sister is who is 14 years younger than me has probably had a cell phone since she was 10 years old and now as a fresh college graduate our parents are still probably paying her cell phone bill. During my Freshman year of college, I went to AT&T to get my first cell phone without a job but I wanted one and I was sure I could pay my bill on my allowance from my parents. The first thing they wanted to do was to run my credit. I quickly found out having no credit history is just like having bad credit. That's when I got my first credit card to build a credit history and to get my first cell phone. My parents had warned me about the credit card trap a lot of college students fall into and their advice was to not get one at all. I knew of all the bad things that could happen if you didn't pay for what you bought on a credit card so even though I got one against their advice, I was responsible enough not to max it out and to at least pay the minimum payment every month without missing a payment. Oh, but I had friends that maxed out several credit cards without thinking twice about it. Back in the early 2000s when we were in college, they were giving out credit card applications and credit cards like free candy. I didn't quite understand the whole interest thing but I eventually got that concept down as well.

Now that we've discussed my introduction into the credit game, I'll let you in on some of the things I learned while building my 19-year credit history. People apply for credit for many different reasons. My initial reason was to build a credit history and that card I got all those years ago as a freshman in college adds to the length of my credit history which is a large contributor to my credit score. Lenders use the age of your oldest account to gauge the level of experience you've had managing credit. This is one of those things that only time can increase. But what you can do is make sure to keep the oldest account you have open and in good standing. The goal is to have good to exceptional credit. When your credit scores are high, you get better interest rates when you finance big purchases such as a home or a car. You also get lower interest rates on other loans and new credit cards. Having good credit is a combination of things such as the type of credit you have, credit age, the amount of money you owe, payment history, use of credit, recent inquiries on your credit report, new accounts, and available credit. One way to increase your credit score is to focus on these areas. If you have maxed out all, most, or some of your credit cards, then the amount of money you owe is high in comparison to the percentage

> ***"Your goal should be to pay off your credit card bills in full at the end of each month and set aside money toward your emergency savings." - Suze Orman***

of credit you still have available at your disposal. The best scenario here would be to pay off some of your credit cards and as you do that, the available credit to you will increase and positively impact your credit score. Your credit card use is how much credit you are using compared to your total limits. It highly impacts your credit score because to lenders, if you have used a great deal of the credit available to you, then you may not have enough credit when you need it and they see this as you being overextended. A good goal would be to keep your credit use below 30%. It is also important to use your credit cards because if you pay them down and stop using them completely, then lenders will close accounts based on non-activity. This could negatively affect your credit score if the card they close is your longest line of credit and also the total amount of available credit will decrease by the amount of that line of credit. A better thing would be to make at least one purchase that you can pay in full every month or every couple of months to keep your accounts active, your balance at zero meaning you incur no interest on remaining balances, and you can increase your number of on-time payments.

Your percent of on-time payments have a high impact on your credit score. So, if you make a habit of missing payments or making payments late, not only are you risking getting additional late fees tacked on to your account but you also are negatively impacting your credit score. There is no better way to show lenders that you are responsible with managing your credit than making consistent on-time payments. Any account that has late payments of 30 days or more risk being reported to the credit bureaus. Excessive late payment will hurt the health of your credit. If making on-time payments is something you struggle with, please sign up for autopay to at least make the minimum payments on all of your bills and credit cards. You can also set up bill pay reminders to keep you on track. I have a recurring calendar reminder to pay bills on each and every one of my paydays.

When it comes to inquiries on your credit report, the less you have the better. Be very careful when someone at a retail store asks if you are interested in seeing if you qualify for their store card. Always ask if they will have to run your credit; this is an important question because some may be rewards cards with no need to run your credit while others can be for a store credit card which would give you a new inquiry on your credit report. You should only apply for credit when you need it and not permit multiple people to run your credit just to see if you will be approved for something. If you do not need a new line of credit just tell them no. When shopping for auto and home loans, there may be times when they have to run your credit multiple times for the same type of loan, i.e. an auto loan with different lenders then that would count as one inquiry as long as it is within a 14-day window. Rule of thumb: do not let people run your credit if you don't need additional credit. Too many credit inquires give lenders the impression that you are applying for multiple lines of credit and that perhaps you are overextended. This also rings true with the number of new accounts you open within a two-year timeframe. Derogatory remarks made by collections that become public record can stay on your credit report for 7-10 years so the best thing you can do is to avoid any from ever appearing on your report. You can do this by keeping track of what and who you owe and by never defaulting on any of your credit accounts or loans with your lenders.

Simply put, having a good credit score comes from paying your bills on time and keeping all of your accounts in good standing for many years. There are three credit reporting agencies: TransUnion, Experian, and Equifax. Although they differ slightly, a good credit score across the board would be around 720. Having a credit score of 800 would be very good or excellent. A huge benefit of having a good credit score is that you would qualify for lower mortgage and auto loan interest rates. Having a good to excellent credit score also gives you the best chances of getting approved for the best credit card offers.

There are two services for credit reports and credit scores that were listed among the best personal finance services of 2018 according to PC Magazine online. They are Credit Karma and WalletHub. Both are online services that notify you when any changes to your credit report occur. This is extremely important in the world of identity theft. Many victims do not quickly notice that their identity had been stolen or new credit cards or accounts were being opened. Utilizing these services or more like them can help you identify and dispute any bogus additions or errors early (Duffy, 2018).

Credit Karma (www.creditkarma.com) is a free website that gives you access to your credit reports and weekly scores from TransUnion and Equifax. It also provides you with information to assist you with improving your credit score; along with a credit simulator tool that shows how doing certain things will affect your credit score. There is also a mobile phone application for this website. WalletHub (www.wallethub.com) is another free website that monitors your TransUnion credit score, gives you your credit report and teaches you useful things about personal finance. WalletHub updates your score daily and also has a mobile phone application that correlates to their website (Duffy, 2018).

SIMPLY DO:

- **Do sign up for a free credit reporting website that gives you monthly updates on your report and credit scores.**
- **Do stop making new charges on existing credit cards until they are paid off (then pay the balance down to zero every month).**
- **Do use your credit cards responsibly by not maxing them out by spending beyond your means.**
- **Do read the fine print. Be sure to read and understand all of the terms and features on your existing credit cards and any you apply for in the future.**
- **Do try to pay your credit card balance in full each month, but if you can't, at least make the minimum payment by the due date each month to avoid late fees and have it negatively impact your credit.**

- **Do pay bills on time, ALWAYS.**
- **Do report lost or stolen credit cards to creditors immediately.**
- **Do check your credit reports periodically for inaccuracies and immediately report errors to resolve any issues.**

POTENTIAL ADDITIONAL INCOME STREAMS

"There are no shortcuts when it comes to getting out of debt." - Dave Ramsey

If you find yourself bogged down in debt or you just want to pay down debt faster, you can explore additional income streams. Maybe picking up a part-time job, turning your hobby into a paycheck, or just finding something that you do well that others seek your advice on could turn into lucrative additional income streams. The benefit of additional income streams is that you can pay more on your debt without having to cutback in other areas of your current budget. I was able to take advantage of a deployment opportunity with my employer that allowed me to work overtime and make additional money on top of my salary at the time. It was a six-month commitment and I was able to break my lease on the apartment I was renting at the time since I would be out of the country. During that six-month time frame, I was not only bringing in additional income but I also saved on approximately 800 dollars a month in rent. That alone was 4,800 dollars which I used to pay down some of my credit cards during those six months. I had approximately 11,000 dollars in credit card debt at the time and I paid all of it off within that six-months. What helped me to do this was that I didn't really need to buy anything while I was on deployment and the recurring bills I had decreased considerably. I was even able to put my cell phone bill on hiatus and lower my car insurance rate because my vehicle was being stored at my parents' house for the duration of my deployment, meaning that my car was not being driven. My solution was a bit extreme and not everyone has the opportunity to take part in a deployment and leveraging it as an additional income stream. But there are certainly other things that you could look into as a way to make more money to pay down debt quicker and to jumpstart your journey to financial freedom.

One thing you can do like I did would be to seek out additional income with your current employer. Ask for a raise, pick up overtime if it is offered. If you are in a commission-based career then work harder at earning more commission, by selling more. Seek out promotions that pay more than your current job. It is possible that there may be nothing available with your current employer. That's why it is important that you make yourself marketable to put you in a better place to seek higher-paying jobs elsewhere. There are also other ways to earn more.

There are a variety of part-time jobs you can get. Some of the more traditional ones include retail and serving or bartending at restaurants and bars. Some other options if you have earned a master's degree or higher you can try to get hired at a local community college, online university, or local university teaching classes in your field of expertise as an instructor. You can also tutor students from grade school through collegiate students if you have expertise in specific subjects. In order to earn more cash, you could sell things of value that you no longer need or use. Own designer bags, shoes, clothes, or formal gowns that you probably have only worn once or maybe twice since you've purchased it? Those would be good things to try to re-sale at consignment stores or on your own at sites like Tradsey, Polyvore, or eBay, to name a few.

If there is a special talent that you have or skillset where others come to you for help or assistance, then consulting on that may be your key to making additional money. I have a couple of friends who were always asked to look over resumes and they started charging for their time and their talents. One friend even helped others edit their interest letters and essays for undergraduate and graduate admissions. What do people ask you to do? I get a lot of financial questions from family members and friends who need help with budgeting and paying down debt. They see that I have managed to do it without being a pauper and they've asked for my help. I've been doing this for the last 11 years and I decided that I can get paid for my consulting services as a financial coach. I hold two graduate degrees in Business including an MBA and I've helped myself and others become more fiscally responsible.

You can also explore the options of freelance work if your passions, hobbies, or expertise are in something that people are interested in, like photography, writing, editing, designing, coding, etc. People will pay you for your services, talents, and passions.

I could go on and on about different avenues for you to take to earn additional money to help you with your finances but what fun would that be? I want to charge you to take some time to think about what you can personally do that would be beneficial to your soul and your pockets. The truth is that the best thing to choose would be something you are passionate about doing or that you actually like to do because that way you would probably stick to doing it, you would be good at it, and it may not even feel like work.

Digital Download of the ***Simpli Financial Guide*** available at:

https://stacihuddleston.com/secure-success-guides/

PROSPERING PROFESSIONALLY

7

SECURING SKILLS

A winner is someone who recognizes his God-given talents, works his tail off to develop them into skills, and uses these skills to accomplish his goals.

- Larry Bird

While there are people who luck out and become successful overnight that definitely isn't the standard. Even when it is perceived that someone is instantly successful, you don't know their story. You don't know their drive, skillset, or the time and dedication they put into becoming successful prior to you even becoming aware of their success. Patience and hard work are two things that you need to possess on your road to success. Sometimes the road may seem easy, but other times, it may seem as if you are climbing uphill and the surface never flattens out. During these times, perseverance is something you also need to possess. Many times, I've felt like I was working hard doing my best for extended periods of time; but it seemed to me in those moments that I was not really getting anywhere. I couldn't see the fruits of my labor and it seemed as if my career was stagnant. But if you just keep going and don't give up, you will reach a point where it will all comes together and there will be a visible light at the end of the tunnel. I kept working hard and I also kept learning to enhance the skills I already possessed while gaining new skills that would be beneficial to me and my employer. I was blessed by others in powerful positions noticing my hard work and dedication and they were able to elevate me into leadership positions and provide me with opportunities to show what I was capable of. I was afforded the chance to prove that I was the right person for the job. Had I given up, stopped working as hard, or started begrudging the process by becoming complacent, those doors would not have been opened for me. You have to stay the course and remain true to you and your work ethic. Never compromise your quality of work because you feel that your hard work is not paying off.

Successful people work hard and they also possess skills that help them to become successful. They try to find ways to improve on their current skills and learn new skills in order to stay relevant and remain successful throughout their careers.

Have you ever thought about where you want to go in your career? What is it that you'd like to achieve? Is your current career field one you see yourself retiring from after working 30 plus years? You may know exactly what you want to do and be in life but I will be completely honest, my idea of what I see myself doing 20 years from now still escapes me. I don't have a clear-cut vision of what that is. I do however have a few things that I can see myself doing, but it all just comes down to which road I decide to travel. Currently, I have 12 years of civilian service with my current employer and I can see myself retiring from the government sector as a Director or Senior Executive if I keep on the trajectory that I'm currently on. The thing about that path is that I am currently single and I have yet to have any children. I see myself being married and having at least one child in the near future, so that would play a big part in the path I choose for my career. I would love the flexibility of the work schedules that are offered at my current job. However, I would have to anticipate that having such a high-profile job might not allow me the ability to take off for field trips, parent-teacher conferences, or having young children who could get sick at any moment. These are real-life concerns that must be considered. Could I do both? Of course, I could. But would I want to? That is the question that I have to answer. Another career that I've been considering is that of a writer. I can see it now; New York Times Best Seller status would be amazing! This option would allow me the flexibility to travel, be a present parent, and it would also feed my passion. The third thing I have been pondering as either an after-retirement career or something I could do to bring in an additional income stream would be to teach at the collegiate level. I'm currently qualified to do so on the undergraduate level or at a community college since I hold two master's degrees. If this was something I really wanted to pursue full time, I'd have to bite the bullet and go back to school to pursue and complete a doctoral program to make the kind of money that I'd like to make and that I have become accustomed to. I have options and you should too!

If you've always known what it is that you want to do for a living for the rest of your life, more power to you. If not take some time to think about it and come up with a couple of things that you are most drawn to. Once you have narrowed it down, figure out what is needed for you to accomplish your ideal career. Some people think that just doing a good job will get them noticed and promoted but there are other factors at play. The main one being professional development. Staying current in your career field by continuing your education to pursue additional degrees or certifications can be extremely important in some positions and careers. Do not become stagnant by doing what you have always done while the world and your career field may be changing around you. In my current career field, I never stop learning, seeking certifications nor allow the systems and software to outgrow me. If you want to be professionally successful, you have to embrace change and continue to develop yourself professionally. Attend industry conferences and seminars. Research what's needed for you to be that Chief Financial Officer or Vice President of Marketing. Even if it is your goal to be a Team Leader or Manager for your current employer, then find out the qualities, attributes, credentials, and background of those who hold similar positions within your organization. Then take the necessary steps to put you in the best position to not only get selected for those positions but to also help you to be successful once you are in them.

I have a friend who wanted to go into real-estate and she pursued her real-estate license while she was working a full-time job. She even took an enhancement course to prepare for the real estate exam in order to give herself the best chance to pass it and to be one step closer to her dream career. She is now licensed and has since sold multiple houses as a supplement to her income. You have to be willing to set yourself up for success not for failure.

You may be wondering how to go about setting yourself up for success? Well there are a list of essential skills that you should work on honing in order to develop a skillset that will aid you professionally in your career no matter what it is today as well as far into the future. What you will realize is that these skills will not only be beneficial to you professionally but also personally in life as well. Most of us have all been on job interviews and have been asked questions pertaining to our ability to multitask, prioritize, manage conflict, delegate, communicate, etc. The reason is because all of these skills are important for individuals to not only have but to also excel at in order to secure their success. These are the skills that people are most familiar with so it is imperative to take the time to strengthen these skills; but there is also a list of essential skills that don't always come to mind. These are the skills that I want to dig a little deeper into. There are three essential skills that I want to focus on that pertain to one's self. These skills can be classified as self-improvement skills; they are Confidence, Balance, & Resiliency.

BUILD YOUR CONFIDENCE

I'm sure you've heard the phrase, "Confidence is Key." That's because it truly is! Having confidence in yourself and your abilities is basically the first of those self-improvement skill you need to reinforce. Stop doubting yourself and your abilities; if you find yourself in constant conflict with what you want to do and what you believe you can do then it is time to start the process of believing that you can do and be whatever it is you want to do or be. You just have to work hard to accomplish it. If you honestly don't believe in 'You' then who else is going to believe in you? Your having confidence gives other people the green-light to also have confidence in you. I know, this is easier said than done, right? Yes it is, but let me let you in on a few things you simply should do to help build your confidence.

SIMPLY DO:

- **Stop thinking about what others think of you and start proving to yourself that you can accomplish the goals you set.**
- **Ask people that you trust what your best qualities are. Sometimes hearing your positive attributes from others can help you to believe them.**
- **Prove that you can do challenging things by embracing chances to do so.**

- **Identify what you know and what you still must learn.**
- **Focus on those things you still need to learn and practice them regularly. They don't say practice makes perfect for nothing. Continuing to do those things you need improvement in, because it helps you to get better at them. It also builds your confidence in not only doing those things but strengthens your overall confidence.**

FIND YOUR LIFE BALANCE

No matter what stage in life you are currently in you have to find the right balance. This is about more than just a work-life balance; all the areas of your life should be in a healthy balance. If things in your life are unbalanced; you may find that you are focused on one area disproportionately to others areas. When this happens you need to prioritize or realign in order to assist in your life's fulfillment and securing success in your life.

When you spend all of your time at work, your home life and family tend to suffer. When you neglect your health that area suffers. If your sole focus is on your family then your social life suffers. It would be nice if there was one universal sweet spot to finding that balance towards living a fulfilling and happy life but the truth is that it is different for each person. There is no one size fits all formula. You have to recognize when you are obsessing over one area and neglecting others in your life. Once you acknowledge this, then it is in your best interest to figure out what you are going to do to fix it. Do that as quickly as possible. Do not let it go on too long because it will results in you sacrificing your happiness and the happiness of those you love. You have to be cognizant of your life balance every step of the way. Who wants to reach their ultimate level of success and be at that pinnacle alone because you've alienated your friends and family along the way? The truth is if you have no one in your corner; you have not reached the ultimate level of success. If you have no one on this earth to celebrate with then you can't truly be successful in every area of your life. You may be successful in your career or in a monetary sense but not in terms of building and fostering relationships and more than likely you are not doing so great with your life's balance.

You have to learn the tools to create order from chaos so that you can maintain balance in your life. Here are some things you simply should do to keep your life in balance.

SIMPLY DO:

- **Keep your commitments. If you have made commitments to date night or attending your child's basketball game then show up unless there is an emergency that comes up. Every so often something unpreventable may come up but do make sure that you are keeping your commitments the majority of the time.**
- **Say no to additional obligations if they are going to cause you to neglect other important things. Don't just say yes out of impulse.**

- **Do plan and stick to your plans and schedule. Scheduling things such as family time, social gatherings, community involvement, business, spiritual obligations, health appointments and other commitments is a way to help balance your life. Make sure that you are planning time for all the things and people that bring you joy. Also plan for those things such as working and professional development that are necessary for your current and future success.**

STRENGTHEN YOUR RESILIENCY

This is a skill that truly develops over time. Life has many twists and turns, setbacks and failures. The key to remember here is it all boils down to how you react to those things when they happen to you. How you respond and recover either strengthens or weakens your resiliency. Do you just give up and quit? Do you stop trying? Do you blame others for your failure? Do you wallow in your failures and setback? If you answered yes to any of these questions, it is time to change that this instant! You must first take a moment to learn from your failed attempts and setbacks along the way. This prevents you from making the exact same choices that will lead you to an identical outcome in the future. Be sure to identify what worked in that situation and what doesn't.

Although resiliency is one of those skills that builds a little bit more day by day; there are things you simply should do to help you to become more resilient in both your personal and professional life.

SIMPLY DO:

- **Train your thoughts & speech to be positive. Optimism comes naturally to some; others have to make conscious decisions to practice positivity. Recite positive affirmations daily. Speak positive things over yourself and your life.**
- **Take some time to write down things you are good at & that you love about yourself.**

- **Surround yourself with trustworthy people. When you face setbacks in life. You want people in your corner that you can talk to, who can motivate you to push forward, who can provide encouragement and gives you strength to get through any storm.**
- **Do accept and be open to change. Change in life is inevitable you can either embrace it or reject it. In order to aid you in embracing change; try to get a clear understanding of what the change is and how it will directly impact you.**

Continue improving upon building confidence, finding a life balance, and strengthening your resilience. Also be sure that you are continuing your self-care even in your professional life.

Digital Download of the ***Top 5 Professional Skills Needed in Your Toolbox*** available at:

https://stacihuddleston.com/secure-success-guides/

PROFESSIONAL SELF-CARE MONTHLY CHECKLIST

Over the next month, try to check as many of these each week as you can:

Professional Self-Care Task	Week 1	Week 2	Week 3	Week 4
Balance your workload and manage your time based on what you need to accomplish				
Plan your day or week				
Take Breaks...Get up from your desk from time to time				
Declutter your workspace				

Professional Self-Care Task	Week 1	Week 2	Week 3	Week 4
Arrange your work area for comfort				
Meet with your leadership regularly for feedback on how you are doing				
Request or volunteer for assignments that are exciting or rewarding				
Set appropriate boundaries with colleagues...but do engage and maintain positive professional relationships				

TABLE 5: MONTHLY PROFESSIONAL SELF-CARE CHECKLIST ADAPTED FROM (NATIONAL ALLIANCE ON MENTAL ILLNESS, N.D.)

8

PROFESSIONAL DEVELOPMENT

An investment in knowledge pays the best interest.

- Benjamin Franklin

I recently participated in a Senior Leader Advanced course at the University of Alabama in Huntsville. My employer paid for my travel and the course in its entirety. Take advantage of as many free training opportunities that your employer offers. I would not suggest you do anything that I would not do myself. Your professional development is essential to you being successful in the professional arena. If it is your desire to continually move up in your career field, then you have to stay marketable. You need to invest your time and sometimes your own resources into staying up-to-date in your chosen profession. Remain competitive with your current employer and also in the industry you work in. The one thing we can count on is for things to change because we know that change is inevitable. There is always a better more efficient way to do something just around the corner. Do not become so complacent in what you already know that you fail to realize that having that mentality will quickly make you obsolete. What does that mean? Well, if someone else can do exactly what you are being paid to do faster, more efficient, and in essence better than you, then you are not really needed to do that job. If the person is a younger person fresh out of college still eager to learn new things, they may even cost your employer less to hire them over keeping you. You are striving to be successful in every area of your life and this one right here is no different. It takes more than just learning your craft, you have to continuously strive to be the best at your craft. You want to be the go-to person that others look to when they have a question or need a solution to a problem. You want to become a subject matter expert in your career field and never stop learning ways to improve your skill sets and continue adding new expertise to your toolbox.

New developments or advancements in technology could alter what you know about your job or even how you do your job. When I first started with my current employer 11 years ago, we used certain systems to perform our job duties but many of those systems were antiquated and eventually became obsolete. They were replaced by newer technology and the workforce had to adjust by adapting to change. You should strive to be one of the early adapters, which was the approach I took. I wanted to be one of the first people to learn the new system and I was. I was a quick learner and I was able to train others on the proper way to navigate and perform tasks in the new system. My leaders made note of this and it has definitely worked to my advantage throughout the progression of my career. There are employees who will complain and be resistant to change but when it all boils down to it, they will still have to learn the new system. It would be a much better use of their energy if they focused more on learning and less on complaining. I understand that all change isn't good change, but when it comes from the top levels of leadership and it's going to happen no matter what, why not roll with it and focus on the positives? That's what I choose to do, and I suggest you should too. If you fail to stay current and fail to add new skill to your toolbox, then you fail to be as competitive as you can be in your career. In order to secure your success professionally, you should strive to be a change agent. Find ways to implement change that will streamline processes, increase efficiency, and make your organization better now and well into the future. Volunteer to participate in surveys or working groups when asked. That way you can have input on the ground level of some issues driving the change in your organization.

If your employer offers to pay for any training opportunities, college courses, or certifications, then you must take advantage of that. My current employer mandates that every employee completes 40 hours of continuous learning training yearly because they are investing in their workforce. These hours are used to refresh skills, add new skills, and to broaden our knowledge base by learning skills from different career fields. Do what it takes to become better at your craft. Becoming a subject matter expert in your chosen career field will play a vital role in your overall professional success.

By day, I'm a logistician, and the course I recently took was a part of the Master Logistician Certificate Program which is the highest certification in my career field with my employer and it is also recognized industry wide. The title, Master Logistician, will allow me to become a part of a select talent pool for senior leaders. I have goals far above where I currently am, so this is one of the ways I am making myself stand out in a crowd. Do not fade into the background. Find trainings and projects that will allow you to shine or be selected over your colleagues when opportunities and promotions become available. I am always up for a challenge and I love learning new things. When new opportunities present themselves, I weigh the pros and the cons; if the pros outweigh the cons, I go for it! I've learned to step out of my comfort zone; it is in those moments that I have grown the most!

> ***"The single most powerful asset we all have is our mind. If it is trained well, it can create enormous wealth in what seems to be an instant." -Robert Kiyosaki***

In addition to focusing on developing yourself by obtaining additional training related directly to your career; there are other non-career specific skills that you can also enhance when it comes to your professional development. Three major skills to help you prosper professionally that you should improve include but are not limited to collaboration & teamwork, leadership, and delegation.

TEAM WORK MAKES THE DREAM ...WORK!

It doesn't matter if you work for someone else or if you are an entrepreneur who works for yourself, you cannot succeed in life if you do not work well with others. Collaboration is an important skill that should be practiced and developed throughout your career. Collaboration is working with others to accomplish a common goal. It is a form of teamwork where working together allows for the flow of shared ideas, additional solutions, and streamlined problem solving. It is very true that you are almost certainly capable of solving problems, launching products, and creating campaigns on your own. However, collaborating with others can help to introduce you to thoughts and ideas that you may not have come up with alone. Often times brainstorming sessions as a part of highly functioning teams can be a catalyst for helping teams reach solutions quicker. The key takeaway here is highly functioning teams. Not all teams are considered to be highly functioning. Some teams can be toxic, unproductive, and even a waste of time. In a highly functioning or high performing team, members are committed to the purpose and goals of the team. Members take accountability for their assigned tasks. Members of high performing teams resolve any dissension or conflict constructively. Since teamwork is something you should be reinforcing you should strive to always be a high performing member of any team. Below is a list of things you simply should do to make sure that you are a high performing team member.

SIMPLY DO:

- **Listen to others. Being overbearing and not allowing others to speak is not a part of being a good team player.**
- **Do your research. Be sure to know the ins and outs of the problem or project you are collaborating on.**
- **Be respectful of opinions of others.**
- **Be able to provide and receive constructive feedback.**
- **Be willing to give and seek input from other team members.**

Being able to work well with others is a skill that will help you get to the place you want to be in life. If your goal is to prosper in life both personally and professionally perfecting this skill will surely help you along the way.

TO LEAD ...OR NOT TO LEAD?

Whether you currently work in a leadership position or desire to work in one it is important to develop your leadership skills. These skills make you a better leader in your career and also in life. If asked what makes a good leader, I could rattle off a number of attributes. Being able to delegate, inspire others, provide constructive feedback, and resolve conflict are the ones that initially come to mind. If you are still trying to figure out what type of leader you'll be simply do these things to become a better leader immediately.

SIMPLY DO:

- Be willing to give and seek input from other team members.
- Clearly communicate your expectations.
- Frequently provide actionable feedback. It will help to improve performance.
- Keep the lines of communication open. Share information with leaders and also share the appropriate information from higher leaders with your subordinates. This includes praise, non-sensitive information, and things that will affect them directly and sometimes indirectly.
- Know your job. No one wants to work for someone that doesn't seem to know what they are doing. Display your expertise.
- Recognize good work and hard workers. When people feel appreciated it increases the morale of the organization.
- Lead with integrity.

- **Do show your appreciation. Say thank you when someone does something nice to assist you whether you asked for their help or not. People like to be recognized and appreciated. You will be surprised how far recognition goes both in your personal and professional relationships.**
- **Do be positive in your interactions with people. If this doesn't come naturally to you then please work on it. They don't say: "you catch more bees with honey" for no reason. Being nice to people, makes them want to be nice to you in return.**

DO YOU DELEGATE?

In the professional arena it is vital that you do not burn yourself out by doing all of the work yourself. Delegating allows you to assign tasks to others in order to complete everything on time. In order to properly delegate you must be able to prioritize tasks. You need a working knowledge of the skillsets of the individuals available to assist in order to properly assign each task to the right person for the job. Delegation is the perfect tool to aide in projects being completed in a timely manner and to allow you the ability to manage an extensive workload. This is a skill that will come in handy throughout your life. It doesn't matter if it is delegating chores for your children to complete or delegating tasks to employees who work in your company. This is a skill that will elevate you and make you much more efficient. Here's a list of things you simply should do when delegating.

SIMPLY DO:

- Frequently provide actionable feedback. It will help to improve performance.
- Assess skill of individuals prior to assigning them tasks.
- Clearly communicate requirements, expectations, and timelines.
- Keep track of everyone's progress without micromanaging. I've found that having a set day and time for weekly status updates usually suffices. This can be provided in a report, meeting, or via email.
- Communicate any changes to the team as they arise.
- Be available to answer questions, explain, or provide clarity along the way
- Do listen actively. Listen more than you speak.

PROSPERING PERSONALLY & PROFESSIONALLY

9

SIMPLY 'SHIPS

The most important relationship you have is your relationship with yourself. Get this right, and you have the opportunity to live, love and work to your fullest potential. So, think successful thoughts, surround yourself with positive people and most importantly, invest in your beautiful self as a means to living a flourishing life.

– Melanie Schilling

The first part of this book focused mainly on SELF and making sure you are the best you that you can be. Loving yourself, taking care of yourself, appreciating yourself, encouraging yourself, and forgiving yourself are all important parts of nurturing the relationship you have with yourself, but those things are also very important in the relationships you build with others. In my experience, it is very seldom that hateful people who are unhappy with themselves have strong meaningful long-lasting relationships with others. Having meaningful relationships can help you on your road to becoming successful.

Relationships are very important and the relationships you choose to form and nurture can play a big role in how successful you currently are as well as how successful you will be in the future. Over the years, I've aligned myself with likeminded individuals all striving for success, setting and achieving goals, and who are ambitious enough to keep striving to accomplish and do more. We don't all think alike and we don't all excel at exactly the same things. You know what, that is perfectly fine. It is important for you to surround yourself with people who challenge you and your opinions and people who introduce you to different ways of seeing the same things and ultimately make you think; they help you to grow. The personal growth one experiences from such relationships is invaluable.

PERSONAL

> ***"Personal relationships are the fertile soil from which all advancement, all success, all achievement in real life grows." -Ben Stein***

Personal relationships contribute to your personal success, those things in your life that make you happy and fulfilled outside of work. Some of the relationships you form are intentional while other relationships you were born into. Usually, your family members are the first people you know. Relationships with your parents and siblings are those personal relationships you inherently form. They don't just materialize because you chose them. Some of us wouldn't change the members of our families even if we were given the option. Others would choose different family members without giving it a second thought. Those familial relationships helped mold you into the person you are today. One thing I'll guarantee is that no matter what type of family you were born into, you can still be successful. Sometimes it can be a little harder to achieve success based on the obstacles you may have encountered while growing up. Maybe you were not born into money, generational wealth, or fortune but those things are still attainable. If you faced childhood trauma or anything else that can prevent you from achieving the level of success that you envision for yourself, then please take some time to research and seek professional help from a therapist who can assist you in healing, letting go of resentment, and forgiving anyone who caused you hurt or harm in your life. For those of you experiencing family rifts and disagreements; if at all salvageable, by all means, reach out and try to mend them. Life is short and there is no guarantee that if you put it off too long that you will get the chance to make amends. Holding on to resentment and grudges benefits no-one involved and honestly it just takes energy away from other areas in your life that you could be focusing on to contribute to your success.

I know that not everyone has families or maybe they do but those relationships are irreparable; but that does not mean that all hope is lost. Family does not always come in the form of blood ties. I've had several friends over the years who have grown into feeling like family and who are closer to me than some blood relatives. You do not get to choose your family but you can choose how you interact with them and whether you dedicate time to nurturing your relationship with them. The moral of the story is that building and nurturing relationships with your family and friends can help in your success. Having a loving caring support system is important to helping you cope with failure and setbacks, to encourage you to keep going, and to celebrate each and every victory.

I am going to be 100 percent honest. I suck at keeping in touch; it does not come naturally to me and I have to make such an effort to stay in touch with some of my family members and friends. I have been truly blessed over the years to befriend people who are phenomenal at cultivating their friendships, checking-in, and staying in touch, in general. They drive me to try to be as good a friend to them in the communication area as they have been to me. By cultivating these relationships with my family and friends, I stay grounded, connected, and frequently feel fulfilled because they allow me to share important aspects of my life with them. In turn, I too continue to be a fixture in their lives no matter if we live near or far.

ROMANTIC

> *"Don't let your focus be so much on how many times you go on a date but how you can build into one another, share and carry each other's vision, complement each other, develop a deeper level of friendship; grow spiritually together and make the little things meaningful. It's beyond the 100% but more about how committed and dedicated you are daily. Love can only truly exist, when you become selfless and focus less on what is in it for you." — Kemi Sogunle*

On the road to success, everyone would like someone to share their goals, their trials and triumphs, and ultimately share the rewards of their success. Love is a choice. Building and maintaining relationships are also choices. It is important to understand that much like professional growth, personal growth is also very important, and it is a continuous process. If you have never taken the time to read the book, "The 5 Love Languages: The Secret to Love that Lasts" by Dr. Gary Chapman, then I highly recommend that you take some time to do so. If you aren't interested in reading the book, then you can skip that and just take the online quiz at www.5lovelanguages.com to find out what your love language is. Essentially, there are five love languages that people use to communicate or feel loved by their partners. Not everyone has the same love language so what you like may not be what your partner likes which throws the old adage of do unto others as you would have them do unto you right out the window. The Golden Rule does not cut it in relationships, period. Now, there is the Platinum Rule that basically says you should treat others how they want to be treated. The Golden Rule is antiquated and implies that people also want to be treated like you want to be treated which is not always the case.

The five love languages are listed below:

A. Words of Affirmation
B. Quality Time
C. Receiving Gifts
D. Acts of Service
E. Physical Touch

What I've come to learn is that what I like and need out of relationships may not be the same thing that my partner needs. Therefore, to be successful in relationships, I need to work at finding out what my partner needs so that I can express my love for him the way he wants to receive it. This is most definitely a two-way street; if you are going out of your way to learn and cater to your partner's needs, then your partner should be doing the same for you in return. Communication is key in any relationship and it is imperative that you have healthy communication habits. Express your needs to your partner and ask the necessary questions to decipher their needs as well. If your needs are not outlandish or unreasonable, then your partner should be willing to do those things that you need to keep you happy. I took the love language quiz and my top two love languages, with only a one-point difference, were quality time and words of affirmation. Those are two requirements I need from my partner and at this point in my life, I won't settle for someone not willing to make time for me or who won't use words and actions to communicate their love for me. You shouldn't settle for anyone who CAN'T or WON'T give you what you need.

I've grown so much as a person and I've tasked myself with becoming a good communicator in my current and future relationships. When I notice something that doesn't work for me, instead of getting angry and lashing out, I take a beat and try to see the situation from the other person's perspective. I then bring my concerns directly to them in a non-threatening way. This is no time to be passive-aggressive. You can be straight forward without being mean. Using terms such as I've noticed, as a result this makes me feel, I just want to get a clear understanding, etc. without raising your voice or having an accusatory tone can greatly improve your communication in your relationships. You cannot control what others will say or how they will respond to you, however, you can certainly control how you respond to them and every situation.

In order to be successful in any of the relationships in your life, you have to be able to communicate your needs, be open to learning their needs, and try to maintain effective communication for healthy relationships. In the romantic realm, know what you are looking for, let that be known, and don't settle for anyone not willing to meet you where you are. I will not lie; I've never been an "okay, let's just see where this goes type of woman" but in my early twenties this is what I kept running into. I was 24 years old and fresh out of a six-year relationship that started in my senior year of high school. I was a fish out of water on the dating scene. I didn't want to say the wrong thing and to be 100 percent honest, I was so naïve when it came to the game that men were running on me at the time. When they would say, "I'm not really looking for a relationship" or "I just want to see where things will go but I'm not looking for anything serious," I'd just say okay I'm not either. In the back of my mind, the more we would hang out and get to know each other, I'd think that we would eventually become an item, a couple, something official. That could not have been further from the truth, and I got a quick lesson in when someone tells you something or shows you who they are then you need to believe them! At 37, I only date with a purpose so I will not be occasionally hanging out with anyone not wanting the same things out of life and a relationship as I do. I will only give my time to the people in my life who are at the same stage, are looking for the same things, have similar core values, and accepts me for exactly who I am. What once took me months on months on years to be able to do before, only takes a few conversations for me to make a firm decision on what is in my best interest. So, my advice to you is do not waste your time with the guy who barely makes time for you, goes days without communicating, or sends the low investment "Hey" text every now and then. If he is inconsistent when it comes to you, trust and believe that he does exactly what he wants to do and he makes time for what he wants to make time for. That just happens to not be you. For those of you who are still waiting to be found by the man God has for you, or if you are a man still desiring to find the woman God has for you, then make a list. Sit down and examine what it is you would like in a spouse. How do you envision your life with them? Are they kind and generous? Are they ambitious and caring? Do they make you feel beautiful or handsome? Do they make you feel safe and secure? Do they feel like home? Think about it, daydream, write it down, and manifest what you want in your future mate. I'm sure you've heard that all before but the other part to it is to make sure you are your best self and work on those parts of yourself that may not be the most pleasing to others in the meantime. I'm super critical and I sometimes get annoyed by the smallest things. I have to continuously work on my faults and keep improving myself to make sure that I am a person that my ideal future mate would be attracted to and interested in. How can I desire an ambitious husband if I'm lazy and complacent? How can I want a fiscally responsible mate when I'm constantly spending more than I make and living beyond my means? I'm not saying that some opposites can't attract or that one of you wouldn't be able to help the other person grow in those areas but I am saying that if you want to be successful in your relationships and marriages then you have to be your best self, a person that someone else wants to be with. Many people are not aware of their faults, but what I am asking you to do is to do the work and work on you.

Once you are the person you are proud of and you are the best version of yourself, then you can be better in your relationships. You can be open to meeting your partner and even be more approachable. About 10 years ago, some friends and I were discussing the different things that can make us unapproachable to the opposite sex. It was brought to my attention that technology may have been killing my approachability. Back then I was extremely addicted to my BlackBerry and all of its applications. I relied on my phone as a security blanket; it was my lifeline between my non-local friends and family. I couldn't deny that more often than not when I was out in public, I was glued to my phone. I was in a new state all alone; my closest friends and family members were at the least a four-hour drive away. I had to deal with my apprehension of new friends and new surroundings. Was it easy? Not at all, but once I was called out, I decided to make some changes. In an effort to change habits that were stifling me from meeting new people and being asked out on dates, I decided to complete a 30-day challenge. This challenge for me consisted of making a conscious effort to refrain from using my phone to view social media, or constantly texting while I was out and about. It was a great challenge that helped me to be more present when I am out alone or with others. What's the point of spending time with friends if everyone is glued to their devices?

If you are in a place that you want to be open to meeting new people and you've noticed that you aren't being approached, try to put your phone away when you are out having dinner with friends, or shopping by yourself. Make eye contact with people, smile and say hello. Give this a try. You will become more approachable because you are not preoccupied, you will start to have more meaningful encounters with others, and you will live more in the moment. This is important in both personal and professional relationships and it can greatly affect your level of success in these areas of your life and your overall success.

PROFESSIONAL

> ***"The most important single ingredient in the formula of success is knowing how to get along with people."– Theodore Roosevelt***

Not only does building and nurturing your personal relationships contribute to your overall success but building and maintain your professional relationships can be vital to your success. Professional relationships play a role in your career. How you reach goals in the workplace, get promoted, and having the support of people that can help you get there can all depend on the relationships you develop with those you work with and for.

In the professional arena, it is extremely important that you try to create and foster professional relationships with your colleagues, management, and customers. These relationships can make or break your success in the workplace. As with any type of relationship communication is key. When it comes to your colleagues, if you work in a teaming environment with shared goals, it is important that the goals are communicated and everyone is aware of who is responsible for each task that will help the team accomplish the ultimate goal. When you build strong relationships with your colleagues, you can count on them to assist you with deadlines and gathering information when needed. If you take time to assist them when they need help; most likely they will be willing to help you in the future. In the long run, if any of your colleagues get promoted or you end up working for or with them in the future, it will be to your benefit to have a strong positive working relationship with them. The reverse is also true if you were not very kind, didn't assist them when needed, or didn't take the time to maintain a positive working relationship; then if they become your boss they would not have a very favorable opinion of the type of employee you are. Now you would have to prove them wrong instead of starting with a clean slate.

From a leadership standpoint, it is important to have great relationships and communication with your subordinates and your leadership team as well. This allows everyone to be dialed into the company's goals and helps with continuity. When there is chaos or confusion, then it could be to the detriment of the team or organization as a whole. When people feel that they play an integral role in the solution, they give more effort and are, in essence, better team members. Keeping leadership aware of any obstacles and abreast of the team's progress helps to build trust which is another important part of building positive professional relationships. Trust goes both ways. Leaders want to have employees they can trust and employees want to be able to trust their leaders. Being kept in the loop and communicating important information builds trust on both sides.

You may work in a customer service field or be an entrepreneur where you are not constantly surrounded by colleagues or management but you have some clients or customers that you need to build strong professional relationships with in order for your business to be successful. Those solid professional relationships are key to recurring clients and returning customers. Customer satisfaction is crucial when you work in a service-driven industry.

There are a number of ways to make sure you are providing great customer service and it starts with active listening. Make sure that you truly understand the needs of your clients. If you are not sure, then ask follow-up questions for clarity or to ensure that you are tracking their needs. Make sure that you are asking the right questions to understand your client's needs and are providing them with the best service. After you feel that you have fulfilled their needs, follow-up with them to see if you have satisfied their request. Word of mouth can be good or bad and that all boils down to the type of experience your clients have with you and your company. Make sure that the word of mouth your company receives is the result of happy customers spreading the word. Those relationships with your clients and customers can be significant to both your short- and long-term success in the business arena.

SIMPLY DO:

- **Do develop your people skills.**
- **Do identify the personal and professional relationships that need some attention.**
- **Do schedule time to build relationships. Carve out 20-30 mins a day to reach out to your family, friends, colleagues and clients. It can be different people each day but do not go too long without circling back to the others.**

Digital Download of the ***Simpli 'Ships Guide*** available at:

https://stacihuddleston.com/secure-success-guides/

10

SIMPLY GOALS

A dream written down with a date becomes a goal. A goal broken down into steps becomes a plan. A plan backed by action makes your dreams come true.

– Steven Covey

I remember back in 2009 one of my best friends, Mechelle, and I met in Cincinnati, Ohio for a SPA weekend to celebrate my 27th birthday. She was living in Louisville, Kentucky at the time and I was traveling from Southfield, MI. I had moved to Michigan ten months prior and it was a much-needed retreat. I had no family in Michigan and although I had made new acquaintances, I didn't have any deep-rooted friendships at that time. They were mainly surface level. Making new friends when you are an adult can be challenging.

We spent the weekend catching up, getting massages, and discussing what our goals were for the upcoming year. My friend surprised me with my first vision board session and I am forever grateful. I don't recall if I was familiar with the concept at the time, but I do know that I'd never actually created a visual representation of what I wanted to accomplish in life until that day. We had magazines, scissors, markers, and glue. We sipped on wine as we mapped out what we wanted the next year of our lives to look like. I know for sure I wanted beautiful natural hair that looked like former First Lady Michelle Obama, I wanted to be able to save a certain amount of money comparable to the salary I had at the time and I also wanted a promotion accompanied by a raise. It's now 10 years later I still have that same vision board on a piece of green construction paper sitting in my closet. Every year I feel a sense of pride as I revisit and revise my vision board for the upcoming year. When you sit down and realize that of the 10 things you wanted to accomplish, you have succeeded in completing five, you cannot help but feel successful.

Over the years, I've evolved and I now create my virtual vision board via PowerPoint, Pinterest, or Dream it Alive. This way, I can have my vision board as the screen saver on all of my electronic devices to include my iPhone, iPad, and MacBook. It is important when manifesting your dreams that they are at the forefront of your mind. Seeing them daily is one of the ways I am continually reminded of what I should be working towards next.

GOAL SETTING

> ***"Setting goals is the first step in turning the invisible into the visible." -Tony Robbins***

It is the end of this current year, the 1st of December to be exact, and I am in the midst of my goal setting for the upcoming year. I usually spend the latter part of December or the early part of January mapping out my goals. This year on New Year's Day, I wrote down my five short term goals for the year in my planner.

1. Pay off my three credit cards to a balance of zero (again).
2. Save at least $5,000.
3. Complete, publish and promote this book I'm currently writing.
4. Lose 20 pounds and keep it off.
5. Travel.

These goals may seem like they are easy breezy but I will tell you that most of them are way harder than they seem. The honest to goodness truth is that even the simplest goal can be hard to attain if you don't contemplate the steps it will take to complete the goal. It's easy enough to tell someone that you want to lose weight, however, if you don't have a plan to change your eating habits or to incorporate more exercise and strength training into the picture, then all you have is an empty goal. Let's stay away from empty goals and try to fashion our goals around the SMART Goal setting principle of creating and achieving success with each and every one of the goals that you set for yourself.

If you are unfamiliar with the SMART acronym for goal setting, then let me inform you. The "S" stands for being specific in your goal setting. If there is ever a time to narrow down what you want to accomplish, it is now! Broad goals such as I want to lose weight are just okay, so I challenge you to be a lot more specific. An example of this would be, I want to lose 20 pounds. To some, 20 pounds may not seem like a lot but to me I felt my best and loved how I looked in my clothes when I was 20 pounds lighter. The "M" stands for measurable. Weight is an easy goal to measure because you can tell if you've met your goal by the numbers on the scale. Other goals can be harder to measure so you have to make sure to write your goals in a manner that makes them quantifiable. The "A" stands for attainable. Are your goals attainable? Something that you personally can achieve? This is an important part and goes hand in hand with the "R" which represents reasonable. It's cool to have the goal for this current year to become a medical doctor but if you are not already in the medical field, have yet to take the MCAT entrance exam to get you into medical school, or if you are not on the way to pursuing that, then your goal is unattainable to you for this year at this moment. It would not be a short-term goal; however, it is one you could reserve for the future and make it a long-term goal. Having a long-term goal that you want to be a medical doctor in the next five years is more reasonable and realistic. A short-term goal that would coincide with that long-term goal could be to pass the MCAT exam and get accepted into medical school within the next year. While everyone needs both long term and short-term goals, it takes a lot of strategic planning, hard work, wherewithal, ability, and intelligence to become a doctor be it medical or otherwise. So, there would need to be multiple short-term goals for you to complete prior to ultimately completing the long-term goal of becoming a doctor. The "T" in SMART is for time-bound. Put a time frame on your goals so that you can measure your progress towards them or alter your plan in order to achieve them if need be. When do you want your goals to be achieved? What is your grace period? When do you have to start kicking it into gear to achieve your goal on time?

Take some time to think about what you want to accomplish and what things you want to achieve that will make you feel successful. Your list may differ from my list and that's okay. Be true to you and list those things that you want to work towards for you, not for others. The things that will make you proud of yourself and give you greater confidence and pride in the person you are becoming.

GAME PLAN

> ***"If you fail to plan, you are planning to fail." - Benjamin Franklin***

Okay, we have our goals, now what? I hope you took some time to visualize your own short and long-term goals and either jotted them down on paper or created your very own vision board that you have placed somewhere you will see it at least once a day if not multiple times a day. The next step is coming up with a game plan to accomplish those things you want out of life.

A few days after coming up with my goals, I added to them. I added deadlines with dates and I planned out the things that I needed to do to make it all happen. These have been revised for the upcoming year.

Goal #1: Pay off my two credit cards to a balance of zero (again). NLT Dec 2020. I've determined that by paying a specific amount each month I can have this accomplished by July 2020 so this gives me a realistic attainable goal and my plan to accomplish this is to pay a specific amount each month. If life happens and something comes up (car maintenance etc.) that I need to spend money on I will still be able to accomplish this by the end of the year.

Goal #2: Save at least $5,000 NLT Dec 2020. This is an attainable goal for me even after the credit cards have been paid off because I took a look at my budget to make sure that I could afford to make it happen. I will have to save a little every month and once the cards are paid off, I can put the amount I was paying towards them into my savings account. The keywords in this goal are "at least" meaning that I can save as much as I can save, but by the end of the year, I would like to have an additional $5000 in my savings account than what the balance is today.

Goal #3: Complete (no later than 31 December 2019), publish (no later than 30 June 2020) and promote (May-

August 2020) this book I'm currently writing. This is where backward planning comes into play. I know the average word count or page numbers of inspirational books so I make sure to keep track of how many I have. It allows me to determine how many words I need to add each day. I use this to plan my writing schedule and I even have an alarm set to write daily at 5:00 pm. This book is a labor of love and it is my way to walk in my purpose by helping others through my experiences. I'm just an ordinary woman from an underprivileged neighborhood trying my best to make God, my family, and myself proud. Some things are taught and most things are learned. What a privilege it is that you are able to get glimpses into the person I have become as a result of the life lessons I've learned along the way. If I can encourage one person to be the best version of themselves, then I would have done what I believe I've been put on the earth to do!

Goal #4: Lose 20 pounds and keep it off by the end of the year. Although there are some people like my cousin, Chani, who can lose 70 plus pounds in a 6-month time frame there are people like me where losing weight takes much longer. Honestly, my willpower is not always what I need it to be. I'm human so I fall on and off the exercise and eating right wagon continuously. I have a goal to work out five times a week in the mornings before work Monday-Friday when the gyms are less crowded. I know that I'm a morning person and I have more success in staying consistent with going to the gym before work than I do after working a nine-hour day. So, I recommend you do what works best for you. I have faith in you. If weight loss, healthy living, or just staying in shape is one of your goals, you've got this!

Goal #5: Travel…This is one of those open goals because traveling is one of my favorite things to do, so this simply means doing more of what you love. If travel opportunities come up that will not stop me from achieving any of my other goals, then I'll do them. Two years ago, this goal was super-specific. I was turning 35 and it was my goal to visit at least five countries in my thirty-fifth year of life, #FiveForThirtyFive, and I did! My last trip was the weekend of my Birthday, in Cuba, I touched down in Iceland, France, Mexico, and Canada prior to my birthday trip but it reignited my passion for exploring new countries and cultures. I have flights booked to visit the countries of Malaysia and Bali for the first time in January 2020. I somehow envision my life being that of a jet setter. I haven't quite figured out how this life of travel will come to be but

I'm optimistic that I will do a lot of traveling with my future husband and children. Each time, experiencing it for the first time with them or through their eyes as they have their first experiences in foreign lands, experiencing exotic cultures, and a variety of foods native to the places we visit. Take some time to focus on what it is that you want to accomplish and the steps you need to take to realize your goals.

REVISITING AND REVISING

Once you have your goals identified and you are working your game plan, it is imperative that you revisit, reevaluate, and revise your goals throughout the year. If your goal was to save $5000 by the end of the year and by March you are already there then maybe you can increase the amount you were planning to save or use the additional funds you were going to put towards savings to snowball your current debt instead. Paying a car, mortgage, or student loan down faster could be beneficial to you being successful in the long run. If you also planned to pay down immediate debt such as credit cards with high-interest rates, then you could take the additional money that you were previously putting into savings to pay more on those bills each month.

That is actually the best-case scenario, you surpassed a financial goal ahead of schedule. But we all know sometimes life happens and there may be times when you are six months into working towards your goals and you may be falling short because you needed to take care of something else. Instead of contributing the monthly amount of 400 dollars you planned to put aside for savings, you missed a couple of payments due to unforeseen circumstances. It's June, and you still have six months left to accomplish that particular goal. You can add up the two payments you didn't make and divide it by the remaining six months to see how much additional you need to contribute the rest of the year to make up the difference. It can still be achieved. In this case, it would be an additional 140 dollars per month. To some, that's a lot of money. I do understand that, but then you need to sit down with your budget, bills, and spending habits to see if there is room to trim the fat so to speak and spend less in order to save more. Do you have a cable bill that is 200 dollars a month and you rarely watch anything other than the local networks? Are you paying for an unlimited data plan on your mobile device but looking at the statistics you don't use very much data on a regular basis? Or do you have a slight addiction to Starbucks, and you are hitting them up for five-dollar gourmet coffees multiple times a week? There are always ways to cut back. It all depends on if you are willing to do so or not. Bing your lunch to work and cook more dinners at home instead of eating out so often. I am a happy hour queen but sometimes it's more fiscally responsible to only accompany your friends and colleagues once a month instead of weekly.

Set up a time to revisit your goals either weekly, monthly, or quarterly. Honestly, the frequency depends on the goal itself. Some need to be revisited more often. If it is a weight loss goal (we all know that that can be a slow and steady race you may not see results right away), but at some point, you may need to change your game plan if nothing at all is changing and you are sticking to the script. Now if the script is too drastic for you to be able to stick to that, it can be reevaluated and revised as well. Visit https://linktr.ee/simpli_s to get your free copy of the Simpli Goals: 12 Month Goal Setting Workbook download and receive tips and tricks to aid you along your journey to becoming your Simpli Successful Self!

Digital Download of the ***12 Month Goal Setting Workbook*** available at:

https://stacihuddleston.com/secure-success-guides/

11

PASSION, PURPOSE, & PROSPERITY

You can only become truly accomplished at something you love. Don't make money your goal. Instead, pursue the things you love doing, and then do them so well that people can't take their eyes off you.

– Maya Angelou

Ever wondered why you were put on this earth? What is it that you are supposed to be doing? Or what could you be doing that would benefit others or better yet the world? These thoughts are on a continuous loop in my head. You have people in the medical profession who always knew that they wanted to save lives. Or you may know the pastor who grew up in church and was called to preach at a very early age. I was not like one of those people. There was a time that I wanted to attend Georgetown University and major in Child Psychology; I actually majored in Engineering for the first three years in college but could never really see myself doing that forever. I had a dream of wearing super stylish suits to work every day and being the Vice President of some marketing or advertising agency with a corner office and an amazing view of some big city. I'm saying all of this to say that I didn't know what I would end up doing; I just kind of corrected course as I went along and ended up in the career that I'm in today. I would have never guessed that I'd end up in the field of logistics. If I'm honest, I didn't even know what logistics was or what it entailed until I was hired as an intern dealing with supply chain management. Indeed, there are people who have known most of their lives what they were passionate about; but on the contrary, a lot of us are still trying to figure it out. I have identified some of the things that I am good at and I've also realized some things that I can do to help others. The key is to find something that you are passionate about that will help others and that you can also make a living by doing. I believe once you find that, you can turn your passion into your purpose, and walking in your purpose can bring you prosperity. It was not until I seriously started writing this book that I started to think that I'd found something I'm passionate about. There is no exact science to being successful but somehow, I managed to get to a place in my life where I truly feel successful and I know that it will only get better from here. I felt led to share my story with others who are still struggling to find their sweet spot in life and to give you some pointers based on my own success, failures, and lessons learned. Writing this book is very therapeutic. It makes me recall the good, the bad, and the ugly. With that being said, I can't help but be grateful that God has brought me so far and it is truly because of him that I am the person I am today! If there was one thing that I would contribute my success to, it would be my faith in God! My personal mission statement is to encourage, motivate, and teach people to believe in themselves and to be successful in every area of their lives. I plan to live out this purpose through my new passion for writing and with God's help it will be a prosperous adventure.

"**PASSION** IS A STRONG FEELING OF ENTHUSIASM OR EXCITEMENT FOR SOMETHING OR ABOUT DOING SOMETHING" (MERRIAM-WEBSTER, N.D.-B).

"**PURPOSE** AS A NOUN IS DEFINED AS THE FEELING OF BEING DETERMINED TO DO OR ACHIEVE SOMETHING OR THE AIM OR GOAL OF A PERSON: WHAT A PERSON IS TRYING TO DO, BECOME, ETC." (MERRIAM-WEBSTER, N.D.-D).

"**PROSPERITY** IS THE STATE OF BEING SUCCESSFUL USUALLY BY MAKING A LOT OF MONEY" (MERRIAM-WEBSTER, N.D.-C).

Being the spiritual person that I am, it has always been my belief that all of us have a purpose for being on this earth. The reason we were put here; a reason to make this world a better place. I also believe that whatever our purpose is will ultimately give God all the glory but that is a different conversation for a different time. Our purpose or our reason for being can sometimes be hard to pinpoint or to determine. Finding things that you are passionate about will lead you to your purpose. You know the things that excite you, the things that you never complain about doing. When you are passionate about something, there is a strong feeling of enthusiasm or excitement that comes along with it. I have a couple friends from childhood who could and still sing like angels. As much as I would love to be able to sing or as much as I like music, it's not my calling. As a young girl in the youth choir at church, I'd say I was tone deaf but that may be a bit of an exaggeration. I was always standing in between the two songbirds who could pick up any key or determine when the intro was over, and it was time to sing. On more occasions than I have to admit, I would start in way too soon, and oftentimes, a tad off-key. It literally got to the point where I'd just move my lips but no sound would actually come out. I dreaded the moments when the choir director would say that something was off or that someone was flat and have each person sing the part solo. I'm still trying to figure out how I managed to get out of that so many times but I guess it was because I was always seated next to two sopranos with amazing voices coupled with the fact that I was never really singing so I was never singled out. Joining the choir was one of those things my mom insisted that I participated in even though it just wasn't my thing. This anecdote brings to light two things. One thing is that not everyone has the same purpose, gifts, or talents, and the second thing it points out is that others may want you to do something, or for you to be something but that may not be what you should become. In my mom's defense, she wanted me to be involved in church and something that provided structure and discipline. She clearly didn't think I'd become the next Grammy Award-winning songstress.

Those young ladies I grew up with are still beautifully singing in some capacity today! One, Leah Joelle, is a solo Gospel recording artist and she is passionate about her purpose to lead others to Christ through her music ministry. She has multiple EP albums, singles, and live recordings. The other young lady, Sequia Chamberlain, has been singing in churches for nearly 30 years and is a part of a female Gospel singing group, Praze 1, which just recorded and promoted their second album. They both have a purpose to give God glory through song, however, they each have a different way of doing it. Maybe your purpose can be accomplished alone or maybe it can be accomplished together with other likeminded individuals who have a purpose that aligns with yours. That leads to the final part of this and that is the prosperity piece. When you are walking and living in your purpose by doing things that you are passionate about and that makes you happy, it can be prosperous. God doesn't want you destitute and if you are doing things that please him and that make this world a better place, he will allow you to be able to make a profit while doing it especially if it is something you've been called to do full time. I have friends who have more than one gift and they are able to start nonprofits while also working in an industry that they are passionate about, both helping them live out their purpose. Take my sorority sister who completed her psychology doctorate approximately two years ago. She is employed full-time as a psychologist who helps people heal from past traumas and live each day by ensuring their mental health. She also has started multiple non-profits and scholarship funds to help others trying to enter into her field or just those who are simply in need.

This chapter on Purpose, Passion, and Prosperity was one that I just had to add to this book. This was such an important chapter for me to cover because the majority of my life I didn't take the time to feed my passions. I went along with the status quo in terms of working a normal job that pays well and that I like well enough. I was always hesitant to step out and explore other things that interested me. I would write them off as just hobbies never truly considering them as things that I could make a living by doing. I admire people who truly allow their passions to lead to the purpose God has for their lives. So often once we realize what our life's purpose is we find that it's not only related to things that we are good at but those things that we love doing, and are passionate about. These are the things that when we are doing them they don't feel like work. If no one paid us to do the things that we are passionate about we would 9/10 times do them for free. Which is what I want to encourage you all to do, something that makes you happy that you enjoy doing! That's what the last couple of years have been for me. Writing this book is one of those things! Starting a Vlog/Blog is another one of those things I truly enjoy doing. If you are wondering why that is, it's because I love to write and I love to help others. I love sharing the knowledge that I've gained over the years in school as well as in life. The best part is that when you are feeding your passions and they lead you to your purpose it can lead you to a life full of prosperity! Imagine doing what you love every single day and making a substantial living doing just that. To me this is the secret to securing your success: finding that sweet spot between your passions and your purpose that culminate in a prosperous life both personally and professionally.

Check out the visual representation in Figure 1 of what I like to call the SIMPLI Prosperity Formula. This is a formula that I've coined that illustrates where your Ability, Passion, and Purpose intersect to create Prosperity.

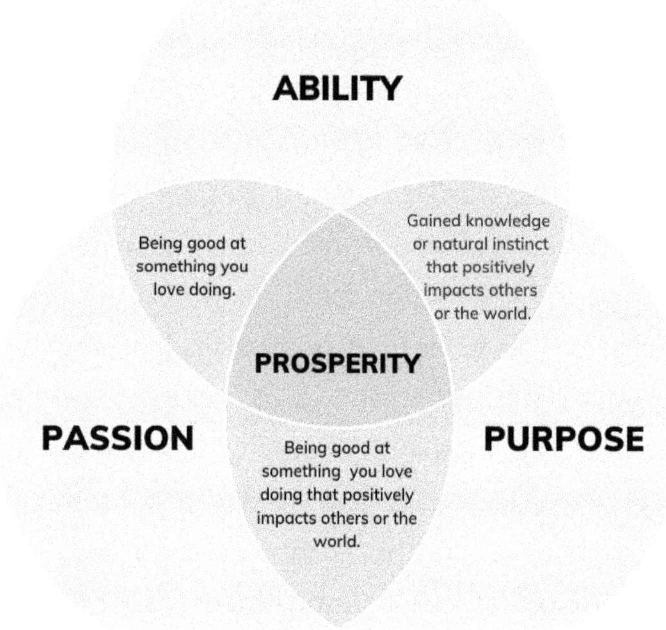

FIGURE 1: SIMPLI PROSPERITY FORMULA

CREATED BY STACI D. HUDDLESTON

Your know-how is represented by your abilities. You being good at doing something you love doing is where your ability and your passion intersect. Your gained knowledge or natural instincts positively impacts others or the world is where your Ability and Purpose align. The final intersection is between your passion and your purpose. This is represented by being good at something you love doing that positively impacts the world.

My purpose and your purpose may differ or they may align. If you are in a place where you are still trying to figure out your life's purpose; what you need to do is some self-reflection. Really think about those things that always bring you joy. Think about what you would do if money was no object and you did not have to work to make a living. Would you travel the world helping to build schools for children in other countries? Would you mentor young girls or boys to teach them how to succeed in life and how to be responsible adults? Below is a list of questions you can ask yourself to help you find out what your purpose is, what you are passionate about, and how those things could lead you to prosperity.

3 P'S QUESTIONNAIRE

PASSION

1. What do you love to do right now?
2. What did you love to do as a child?
3. If you could do one thing for the rest of your life, what would it be?
4. If you could be one person, who would it be and why?
5. What are your goals?
6. What do you do with most of your time?
7. What are your hobbies?
8. What are your talents?
9. Can you combine any of your hobbies, talent, and loves?

PURPOSE

1. Do you love what you do in your current job or industry?
2. Do you daydream about doing something else?
3. If money were no object, what would you be doing? Where would you be working?
4. What motivates you?

PROSPERITY

1. How can you turn any of the things you are passionate about into a business?
2. How can you make money by living in your purpose?

Digital Download of the ***3 P's Questionnaire*** available at:

https://stacihuddleston.com/secure-success-guides/

12

SIMPLY NETWORKING

The richest people in the world build networks; everyone else is trained to look for work.

–Robert Kiyosaki

The concept of networking is not new; it really boils down to building and maintaining relationships with people that can help you in so many ways and that you can help in return.

"NETWORKING: THE EXCHANGE OF INFORMATION OR SERVICES AMONG INDIVIDUALS, GROUPS, OR INSTITUTIONS; SPECIFICALLY, THE CULTIVATION OF PRODUCTIVE RELATIONSHIPS FOR EMPLOYMENT OR BUSINESS" (MERRIAM-WEBSTER, N.D.-A).

Networking may not come naturally to you. However, whether you are an introvert or an extrovert it is something that you need to become familiar with. While networking isn't a new concept, since it became a household name in the 2000s. There have always been people in the same industry meeting up and having conferences to meet others in their career fields. They use these opportunities to build new business relationships that could potentially help their level of success and longevity of their careers. You need to build mutually beneficial relationships where your strengths, connections, and experiences can be brought to the table and those you are networking with can also bring theirs to the table. This will allow both parties leverage when needed. The truth of the matter is that your network makes you stronger! In a professional arena, knowing people in different departments of your organization can help you answer the tough questions, speed up processes, and allow collaboration to solve problems. Just picking up the phone and calling someone in your network can make all the difference and sometimes save you countless hours of research, freeing up time for you to focus on other tasks. I have a colleague who was a fellow intern 11 years ago when we started with our employer who was the point of contact responsible for granting system access. A lot of the systems we work with will deny your access if you go too long without accessing them. I have called my fellow intern classmate to ask him to restore access for multiple people on within my Branch and even myself over the years to speed up this process. What could take a day or more takes a matter of minutes or hours because of my network. I can call on many of my fellow colleagues who I've interned with, taken a course with, or worked with in some capacity over the years to assist with projects, getting stuff done, or to point me in the right direction of the individuals who can assist.

Whether you are a people person or not, it is imperative that you continuously work at making connections and fostering relationships on your road to being your Simply Successful Self, because it is not always what you know but a lot of times, it is who you know. A couple of years ago, I was enrolled in a professional development leadership course where I was one of the 25 leaders and future leaders from all across the United States and even parts of Europe. The course was not just about leadership and best business practices but networking was a huge added benefit of that class. Every senior leader that presented kept hammering in how important it was for us to network; by finding out everyone's specialties so that we would be able to call each other throughout our careers when we run across something that falls into one of their expertise. It's important to engage with people and find out what they know and what they are good at; this by no means is one-sided. Let them know your background and what you are a subject matter expert in. Let them know that you welcome their calls and emails and that you will do your best to give them an answer or point them in the right direction of a person who can be of assistance when they reach out to you.

Participate in office outings, happy hours, and holiday parties. I've run across people in my career who never participate in these functions but they fail to realize that when people are out of the office setting, they often still talk about work-related topics and even make some major decisions. If you aren't present, you literally have no input in some of those decisions that may affect you. To leadership, you are viewed in a more positive light when you participate because it shows that you are a team player which is a great trait to have when they are looking to promote leaders that they will be working with directly. Do not miss out on an opportunity because you do not realize the importance of networking in both your personal and professional life.

On a personal note, I have friends and family members who are medical doctors, lawyers, psychologists, educators, CEOs, entrepreneurs, etc. and they are all just a phone call away if I have a question. If they don't have the answer, they can refer me to someone in their networks better suited to answer the question and to assist me. I've had friends also call to get advice from me on a myriad of things, however, the most frequently asked questions I receive are related to finances.

When these types of professionals are in your friends and family's networks, they don't charge you for simple questions here or there or to give you a little advice. A person who is successful in life doesn't know everything, but they know how to get the answers or the right person to solve the problem. A major key to being successful in life is to build a network because your network makes you stronger. Networking is not confined to face-to-face formal settings; it can take place anywhere and even online. For example, you always go to the same Starbuck on your way to work and you always see the same person while you're there. It will not hurt to introduce yourself and ask if they work nearby. You never know who you'll meet or if you two can build a mutually beneficial relationship romantically or professionally. It does not have to be hard and you don't have to overthink it. Another example could be where you are doing some Saturday Morning shopping at your local bookstore and notice you and someone else are both perusing the real estate section. Introduce yourself and ask if they are in or looking to get into the business. You could already be a realtor and they may be actually looking to buy and want to do their research first. Hello new lead and potential referrals down the road! Invest in some business cards so that you are always prepared when a networking opportunity presents itself.

Networking can also take place online by following like-minded individuals, those who inspire you, or those from your industry. Start engaging them by commenting on their post, sending them a message, or posting content that they are interested in; this can be a starting point to networking with those individuals. It is important to have an online presence that is true to your personal brand in order to build a following that allows you to network more effectively.

SIMPLY DO

- **Do prepare an elevator speech, a brief intro into who you are and what you do. It should be 20-30 seconds. You never know who you may run into. Practice this until it becomes second nature and you can confidently speak it to anyone.**
- **Do follow-up with people you've met at a networking event, or that you randomly exchanged information with.**
- **Do listen. Listening is so important when it comes to networking because you can learn how you all can help each other out in the future. Listen and learn.**

Digital Download of the ***5 Step Guide to Simpli Networking*** available at:

https://stacihuddleston.com/secure-success-guides/

13

SIMPLY BRANDING

Banding is something that comes to mind when you think of businesses or companies but not as often when we think of ourselves. We live in a day and age where it is not only important for businesses to have a brand identity but for individuals to have a personal brand as well. If you are slightly behind the curveball when it comes to branding yourself, you should take the time to identify your personal brand. What is your brand? What do you want people to think when they see you or hear your name? What is the image you want to portray to those you meet? At any networking event, you want to present your best self. We've all heard the adage, "you never get a second chance to make a great first impression." This is so true unless the person doesn't remember you at all, then that obviously isn't a good sign either. You want to be memorable, and whether you are looking for new business from an entrepreneurial standpoint or looking to get contacts for potential employment. It does not take people a long time to size someone up. They can get a sense of if they like you are not within the first few minutes of meeting you. You want to help shape the narrative and intrigue them to want to know more. You want the people you meet to be interested enough in you to want to learn more from and

The keys to brand success are self-definition, transparency, authenticity and accountability.

- Simon Mainwaring

about you from your very first encounter in person or on social media.

Your brand distinguishes you from the competition, it gives you an edge when it comes to someone remembering you, hiring you, or reaching out to you in the future. The truth of the matter is that we all have personal brands whether you know it or not. The colleague who is always late to work, never completes his projects on schedule and is overall a bad employee, has a bad brand and reputation because when people think or speak of them it's not in a positive light. They associate those traits to that individual. Your key to success is to have great qualities attributed to your name. It is my hope that my colleagues, friends, and even strangers think of me as a hard worker, who is consistent, and a leader who motivates and encourages her team. I am not telling you to lie to the people or to create a false narrative or a brand that is nothing like you; I am however telling you that you need to create a brand that is representative of who you are, who you desire to be, and who you are constantly striving to become.

Your brand extends further than in person. Your social media presence also gives people an insight into your brand

and you should be authentically who you are in person and on social media; they should align. You don't want to come across as an arrogant jerk on social media but portray a down-to-earth sweetheart in person. It doesn't match and it isn't authentic. I truly believe people can sense when you aren't being your true self. Take some time to edit your digital presence once you've identified and cultivated your personal brand and professional expertise. Update and maybe revamp your Facebook, Twitter, Instagram, and LinkedIn accounts to make sure they are all presenting you in the best light because those things have a way of lasting into eternity. Delete unflattering content that you wouldn't feel comfortable with a potential employer or client seeing. Add a privacy setting that prompts you to approve every post that you are tagged in and be cautious of what you accept. Potential employers seek out your digital footprint prior to hiring you. Yes, they use Google too! If that's not enough to make you reassess some of the things you have floating in cyberspace or tighten up your privacy settings, then real-life instances where people have been fired from their jobs over insensitive things they've posted should do the trick. Be purposeful in what you share online. This is not to say that you can't share personal stories or information on your social sites because having content that is a good mix of personal and profession allows people to relate and see both sides of you. You can get interviews, jobs, speaking engagements, partnerships, and collaborations if you have a strong online presence and personal brand. All of those things can aid in you becoming successful.

You can't keep people from having bad opinions of you, but you can keep them from being right! There isn't anything you can do to change the way a person initially perceives you, however, you have the power to be the best person you can be. Strive to be the hardest worker. Pride yourself on being the most loyal. Work hard at being the most compassionate, and never stop trying to be the most trustworthy person you can be. It's all about your character, are you proud of your character? You should be! You have the ability to grow into the person you were destined to be. It does not matter if people's perceptions never change because you know that even though they perceived you to be a certain way you may know that their perceptions can't be further from the truth. Be the best version of you and your brand will improve right along with you.

Your brand is a gateway to your true work. You know you are here to do something - to create something or help others in some way. The question is, how can you set up your life and work so that you can do it? The answer lies in your brand. When you create a compelling brand, you attract people who want the promise of your brand - which you deliver. - Dave Buck

Here are some questions to think about to help you with identifying your personal brand:

- What is your personal mission?
- What qualities do you want to be associated with you?
- What makes you different or stand out?
- What are you passionate about?
- What is your purpose?

Digital Download of the ***Simpli Branding: Determining Your Personal Brand Workbook*** available at:

https://stacihuddleston.com/secure-success-guides/

14

SIMPLY STYLE

Successful people consistently put their best "self" forward.

- Lorii Myers

A lot of people want you to think that appearance has no merit in how successful you are. In my opinion, that can't be further from the truth. People judge you by how you look and whether you do it intentionally or not, you also judge people or make assumptions based on first encounters or seeing someone for the first time. It isn't until you speak with the person or have a conversation that you determine if your snap judgments are accurate or completely off. I'm going to give you a scenario. You are an entrepreneur who is looking to hire a website designer for yourself. You reach out to a local agency to who sends you the contact information to two individuals. You call them to set up interviews for the following day. They show up at the same time, and while they both appear to be the same height, ethnicity, and have similar features. The only visible difference between the two potential web designers is that one is well put together, wearing a suit and a tie, tapered hair and the other looks disheveled, hair long, wild and is wearing a pair of tattered jeans and a sweatshirt with visible holes. If both of these candidates have similar experiences and credentials, who are you hiring? I'm personally hiring the guy who looks like he put effort into his appearance before coming to the interview. People want to work with people who care about their appearance and who will be able to represent them and their company well.

PERSONAL

"A girl should be two things: classy and fabulous." - Coco Chanel

Your personal style speaks to who you are and should represent the person you are presenting to the world. I've been cultivating my personal style for years. Many of my friends can pick out a "Staci" dress when they are out shopping or if they see a particular style on someone else. By no means am I boring but I can be a little predictable because I like what I like, and I know which styles flatter my body. It is Simply my Signature Style because it is distinctive to me. My personal style is a mix between classic and modern. I tend to stick to neutral colors and wear trendy pieces here and there to enhance the wardrobe that never really goes out of style. In essence, I want my style to portray the picture of class, sophistication, and confidence. This is a major key: just because it comes in your size does not mean it will look good on you. There are some trends I steer clear of and there are others I embrace. Your style should be distinctive and authentically who you are. If you are dressing for other people, then stop doing that now! I'm not going to feed into the stereotype that all women love shopping, shoes and handbags, but I will say that I am a woman who loves to shop and mostly for shoes and handbags. Honestly, I know women who hate to shop, despise trying things on, and they'd rather be stuck in a predicament where they have to wear the same things all the time just to avoid shopping.

Look, I like nice things and I can also be frugal. I'm not trying to get anyone to break the bank, but on your road to success, I believe that you should invest in a wardrobe that suits you, one that leaves a great impression, and one that makes you feel confident. When you look good, feel good, and are approachable, you'll realize people treat you with more respect and are overall nicer to you. If you have no clue where to start, I want to give you some pointers on some things you should use to build your wardrobe. There are items that are worth a splurge; you can spend a little bit more on them because they will last you for a long time and you will definitely get your money's worth out of them because you wear them frequently. These items are your investment pieces or the must-haves for your closet. These investment pieces should be multi-functional; they can take you from day to date night, boardroom to bar, and everywhere else in between.

Below are some of my Simply Style Staples:

1. Leather Handbag - You need to invest in a nice one that is big and sturdy enough to carry all of your essentials for work, but it is chic enough to carry once you leave the office. It should be able to withstand everyday wear and tear. Pick a neutral color black, brown, gray, or navy. Once you have the neutral colors down, it's okay to purchase a non-traditional color. However, I would not recommend splurging on yellow, turquoise, pink, etc. handbags though because the chance of you carrying them year in and year out is slim. The ones you splurge on in the neutral color will probably be carried for many years as long as it is in a traditional shape that is timeless.

2. Classic Jeans - A pair that fit just the way you like them with no rips or cutouts. You can add those to your wardrobe but they aren't a necessary staple. Invest in a dark wash denim and a black pair; they can be worn in nearly any setting and can be dressed up or down.

3. A Little Black Dress (LBD) - Invest in a figure-flattering dress that can be worn alone, with a blazer, with flats shoes, or with heels. It should not be a mini dress. I'm actually loving the midi length these days that falls right at your calves if it is a fitted dress. You are looking for an all-black dress that can be worn to happy hour, a cocktail party, a wedding, or just to dinner.

4. A Sensible Leather or Patent Leather Pump - You should invest in a closed-toe pump in the color black, navy, or nude with a sensible heel height. When I say sensible, I'm referring to a shoe that you can walk in and that will be comfortable for you to stand in for an extended period if you don't have anywhere to sit when you arrive at an event. It's far better to splurge on a comfortable pair of shoes than constantly complaining about your feet hurting or not being able to enjoy yourself because your feet are in pure agony. I'll be honest I've also splurged on shoes that are nowhere near comfortable but are sexy as all get out and I choose carefully where I'll wear them. I've invested in getting the soles redone and the toe bed stretched all in an effort to make them comfortable to no avail. So, at this point, I wear them when I know I'll have a seat, or I will not have to walk or stand for an extended period. You know when you are valeting and being dropped off at the door! Aside from that, have fun with your shoes. But if you do not have the staples don't overdo it by spending an astronomical amount of money on trendier pairs.

5. A Chic Flat Shoe - No, I am not referring to the CROCs of old. I think they have redesigned CROCs over the years but I'm not sure I'd ever recommend a pair. I mean comfortable flats that you can slide on with ankle-length pants, a skirt, dress, or with a pair of jeans. Think more in lines of a ballet flat. Again, let your first pair be in a neutral color of black, brown, navy, tan, or nude.

6. A Classic Black Blazer - I recommend Black being the first Blazer you own but you can get any Neutral color such as navy, brown, or tan. This can dress up jeans, be layered over a dress, worn with a skirt, or be added to slacks for a dressier option.

7. Tee Shirts - You should invest in both long and short sleeve tee shirts in white, black, and maybe gray. You want the ones made out of a nice soft fabric and not the ones that came in packs of three undershirts your parents made you wear as a child.

8. A White Long Sleeve Button Up Blouse - You can get multiple colors but white is a staple and you should have multiple white blouses. It's okay if the white blouses in your closet differ in style but they can all be worn in the same manner. You can layer with a cardigan or blazer, wear them with just jeans, slacks, or a skirt.

9. A Pair of Black Pants - Pretty much any pair of black slacks will do here. I am very partial to the pencil pants that are relaxed at the hips and thighs but skinny as they go down and stop at the ankle. I like them because they can be worn with heels, flats, booties, or taller boots because they fit nicely into the boots. If you like the fit of boot cut or straight-leg pants, then get the pair you like best.

10. A Cross Body Purse - You can get a cross body purse with straps that come off or that can be tucked in. It can double as a clutch for a night out. Cross body purses are good when you go shopping or when you just do not feel like carrying around a heavy purse. I've recently been carrying them a lot lately so I can fit it in my huge work tote; it cuts down on the number of bags I have to carry into the office. You'd probably get the most wear out of a neutral color.

11. A Skirt - You should have a modest skirt that falls below the knees and can also be work or church appropriate if need be. I'm into the midi length that falls at your calves but as long as it is below the knees it works.

12. A Cardigan - A cardigan is a good layering piece and coming from a cold-natured person who is always cold, a cardigan defiantly comes in handy. Cardigans bring outfits together much in the same way that blazers do without giving an overly professional vibe.

****Bonus****

13. Pearls - I'm not big on jewelry but I always love having pearls to class up any outfit. Whether it's a single strand, multiple strands, long or short, costume or real, they all work. A pearl necklace is a piece of jewelry you can splurge on because like many of the pieces mentioned above, they are classic and timeless. My grandmother wore pearls, my mom still wears pearls and I too love my pearls.

INSPIRATION

If you are still in the process of polishing your signature style, you may need a little style inspiration. Once you have the basics, let's think of inspiration. You have the freedom to experiment a little to see what you like and dislike; what fits your body and what absolutely does not; and what makes you feel comfortable and what makes you self-conscious. These all lead to whether you will feel confident or not. Have you ever seen a purse in a magazine, on a celebrity, or a random person that you really liked? Think of the celebrities you see out and about being photographed by the paparazzi; is there one in particular that you think always looks nice no matter where they are going? Identify a few whose style you really like and are drawn to. Are there women that you run across in your everyday life that you often find yourself admiring their wardrobe? What about on social media...do you follow anyone who dresses the way you wish you could dress if money was no object? You can honestly get inspiration from anywhere. Think about what in particular you like about each of their styles or outfits. Is it because they always wear bright colors or you like that it is more subdued earth tones?

I get a lot of my style inspiration from Pinterest. I've either liked or searched for something and now similar items and styles pop up in my feed. If you've never used Pinterest, I highly recommend it for inspiration on any and everything. Okay, maybe not everything, but I surely can't come up with one thing I haven't used it for. There are recipes, workouts, motivational quotes, affirmations, fashion, art, and so much more.

Back in the day, I loved the wardrobe of Joan's character played by Tracee Ellis Ross on the show "Girlfriends." My style current style inspirations come from characters from these TV shows: "Being Mary Jane," "Scandal," and "Suits." I love how Mary Jane Paul (Gabrielle Union) dressed in Season 4 when she moved to New York City to film Morning News. To be honest I've always liked her style, but it really evolved once she moved from Atlanta to New York. That's something to keep in mind. Your style can be fluid; it doesn't have to stay the same once you have decided what it is. It's a living thing. It can change based on where you are in life, where you live, the kind of work you do, or for any reason for that matter. Mary Jane's New York Fashion was #GOALS and gave me so much inspiration. She wore a lot of form-fitting (not tight) midi dresses which I love! She also experimented with bold colors. Her looks could be worn to work, happy hour, or even church. Her style included modern suiting, versatile separates, and chic dresses. Gabrielle Union partnered with New York & Company to create a Being Mary Jane inspired clothing line and I have definitely found a few pieces that fit perfectly into my signature style.

My next style inspiration came from the character Olivia Pope (Kerry Washington) on the ABC drama "Scandal." Her style was polished and professional. It consisted of muted colors and streamlined silhouettes, meaning feminine cuts and impeccable tailoring. There was always a statement coat, power suit, or waist-cinching outfit which are all things I admire and am inspired by. When my go-to store, The Limited, announced that they were partnering with Kerry Washington and her Scandal costume designer, Lyn Paolo, to bring the Scandal Collection, I was ecstatic. Two of my all-time favorites collaborating was music to my ears and they did not disappoint. When I say my go-to store for almost everything in my closet especially for work and church came from The Limited, I am not exaggerating. I was devastated when they closed all of their stores out of the blue in 2017. I did rack up on some incredible sales and got enough pieces to last me a while, but I still haven't found a go-to store to replace them years later. Both "Being Mary Jane" and "Scandal" series have concluded and are no longer on the air, so I am on the lookout for more style inspiration.

The last show that really inspired my style was "Suits" which airs on USA. Jessica Pearson (Gina Torres), Donna Paulsen (Sarah Rafferty), and Rachel Zane (Meghan Markle, Duchess of Sussex) all had enviable posh and professional style wardrobes. They worked in a Law office on the show so although they all had a very professional wardrobe, they found ways to stand out. Jessica wore mostly muted colors like black, white, grey, and blush. She also experimented with interesting shapes with her jackets, dresses, and blouses like unusual necklines, dramatic sleeves, and peplum jackets. Donna mostly wore shift dresses that were slim-fitting and directional dresses that had fresh silhouettes and modern cuts. Rachel's look mostly opted for a high waist pencil skirt, a blouse, and a pair of heels. This combination gives off a figure-flattering polished and professional vibe and is more business casual.

My style is a mix of polished, professional, both colors and neutrals, sometimes trendy with sprinkles of edgy. It's Simpli Staci! Find a style that fits you, and have fun doing it. Style is a form of self-expression, don't be afraid to be you in both your personal and professional wardrobes.

EDIT YOUR CURRENT CLOSET

Now that you know what staple pieces you need and you've found a little inspiration, it's time to edit your current wardrobe. Go through your closet first to see what fits and what doesn't. If it does not fit, then get rid of it. I remember when I use to carry the span of three sizes in my closet for when I was my average size of a 6, my slightly larger size of an 8 and my smallest size of a 4. I knew that I was never really going to get back to that size 4 and I had to get used to the fact that my new average size was a size 8 and my slightly smaller size was a size 6. Depending on the article of clothing, designer, fit, or the season, I'm somewhere between a size 6 and a size 8. I've come to terms with that and now I buy my correct size. I know what it's like to hold out hope that you will lose all this weight and be able to fit your skinny clothes again and I have no doubt that if you put your mind to it you will succeed at that and meet your weight loss goals! But if it has already been years since you were that size, let's be realistic, those clothes may no longer be in style. So, once you get down to your goal or smallest size, then you can buy updated pieces in your new size. Hey, if it makes you feel better, maybe keep one dress that is timeless not trendy and a pair of jeans in your smaller size for motivation. Get rid of the rest and focus on looking the best you can in the size you currently are now.

Find the staple pieces you can find out of what you have in your closet now, then make a list of the things you still need to get. Keep the items of clothing that look good on you that you've received compliments wearing and that makes you feel confident. Don't forget to keep your style inspiration in mind while you are editing. Maybe ask a friend who you know will be honest and whose opinion you value to help you through this process. Turn on some music, pour up some wine or champagne (I'm more of a Champs kind of girl), and just go for it! In order to prevent your friend from interjecting too much of his or her personal style into your wardrobe, show them some of your style inspiration before you get started.

THINK MULTIPURPOSE

Now that you have decided what from your closet you are keeping and what you are giving away, (if it's presentable, clean, and could benefit someone else then donate it), you have a better idea of what you need to complete this personal style haul. There are two keys here to not breaking the bank. The first one is to think multifunctional when it comes to your additional purchases. I buy dresses that can be worn to church with a cardigan, to work with a blazer and to happy hour once the blazer comes off. This will not be the case with each and every dress but do find pieces that can be worn in many ways to form many different looks. Make sure you pick items that are versatile so that you can get more bang for your buck. The second key here is that you do not have to splurge on everything. To be honest, I buy camisoles from Forever 21 for around two dollars each but I'll splurge on a designer handbag. Why? Because I can purchase camisoles a few times a year and my purse will last me many years. If you splurge on your staple pieces that are good quality, you won't have to continue to purchase them over and over again. I tend to stick with neutral colors when I'm splurging on a bag instead of going for the trendier options, colors or patterns because I will get more wear out of neutral colors. Now, once you have all the neutrals down and if you have the money (not credit) to pay for those expensive pops of color or one of a kind pieces, then I say by all means go for it! The same goes for nice designer shoes. Once I had a pair of black pumps and a pair of nude pumps, I was able to start branching out. I always look for a sale when making these types of pricey purchases and often times I save up to get them.

ACCESSORIZE

Lastly, I recommend that you use accessories to bring out your personal style especially with your staple pieces. I'm not big on jewelry every day but I do love the look of a statement necklace. Most days, the only jewelry I wear is a pair of post earrings and my apple watch. Sometimes, I'll add a statement necklace but I'm still wearing my posts earrings. If I wear dangling earrings, then I'm more than likely not wearing a necklace at all. I'm simpler and more classic when it comes to my jewelry unless I am really trying to dress my look up. If you like a pair of earrings that are doing something or at least that dangle like my lovely mother who has bought me more pairs of hoop earring than

I can count, then go for it. If you like to accentuate your outfits with skill scarves or broaches then, by all means, do you! Use your accessories to bring out more of your personal style.

The accessories I focus on to bring out my personal style is usually my shoes and my handbags. Those are also most times my investment pieces and so they can stand alone and be chic and sophisticated. My style in a nutshell is simplicity, classic, and sophisticated.

How to stay fashionable and not spend a fortune:

- Find your inspiration and shop around to find the best deals for each piece.
- Browse the sale and clearance sections of your favorite stores.
- If there is a coupon or promotion code, find it and use it.

PROFESSIONAL

> ***"Dress shabbily and they remember the dress; dress impeccably and they remember the woman." - Coco Chanel***

DRESSING FOR THE JOB YOU WANT

The dress code for my job has been business casual since I began. I've always stepped it up a notch and I usually wear a blazer daily so I tend to dress business professional like most of the executives and senior leaders in our organization who wear suits and ties on the daily. The directors and top leaders don't even wear jeans on casual Fridays. I adopted this mentality early on as an intern and I suggest you do the same. Allow people to visualize you in that role you envision yourself in the near future. How you present yourself can hugely impact your career and your overall success. Take pride in what you wear and others will definitely take notice.

PROFESSIONAL STAPLES

> ***"Simplicity is the keynote of all true elegance." - Coco Chanel***

It is important that your professional wardrobe matches the dress code of your employer. The dress code in my organization is business casual which means that it's less formal than business professional, but it should still give off a business vibe. For men, a jacket or tie isn't mandated under business casual and for women a suit jacket is not required. Some things that fall into this category are slacks, skirts, button-up shirts, dress shoes, heels or flats for women, but not athletic shoes or thong sandals (flip flops). This can vary by location; some may include khakis (not cargo pants) and polo-style collar shirts can be added to the mix.

It's important to have some staple professional pieces for work if you work in a business casual or any professional environment such as:

- A blazer (black, navy, or gray)
- Slacks (black, navy, or gray)
- A suit that can be pants or a skirt (Black or Navy); my suggestion is if there are pants and a skirt option available then you should buy both.
- A white button-up shirt or blouse
- Skirts
- Sheath dress in a neutral hue

- Classic heels (black, navy, or nude)
- Classic chic flats (black, navy, or nude)
- A structured leather tote in a neutral hue

Many of your personal and professional staples will be the same so you will not have to double up on them.

INCORPORATING YOUR SIGNATURE STYLE

When I first entered the workforce, I was teaching on the collegiate level and I found myself intentionally trying to look older to be respected by the students who were only a few years younger than me at the time. I would wear sweater sets and my glasses every single day. It took my cousin, Nikky, the ultimate fashionista with a personal style envied by many, to sit me down and get me together! "This isn't you; this isn't even your style." Since then I've found ways to incorporate my personal style into my professional wardrobe. You have to dress for success, but be you while doing it! Dress for the job you want, not the one you currently have. Take pride in your appearance and let your personal style shine through. Who said dressing professional has to be boring? There are ways to be you and infuse some things that are different or that are not traditionally thought to be professional in your work attire. Take, for instance, color.

I swore off colored pants somewhere around high school, but I've since realized the error of my ways because I was limiting my work wardrobe to the traditional neutrals. A solid vibrant color pair of pants, be it red, green, or even yellow can still fit into the professional realm. The trend is definitely back and many people, myself included, are rocking them in a super chic way. I was that person who would look at someone else and think, "They can wear those red pants, but I can't pull it off, especially in a professional environment." I'm sure you've seen a bold pant done in a chic way and you've also probably seen it done in a very unflattering way. One day, I decided to step out of my normal box and spice up my attire for work. Back then, I played it safe with my work attire even though I would take the risk with my personal style. I would stick to the basics by wearing only navy, black, brown, or gray when it came to pants for work. Now, I wear pants in colors and patterns, and I pull it off every time. It's Simply a Do!

How to wear a bold or patterned pant in a professional setting:

- Pair them with a blazer to give it a more professional feel
- Make sure that the other pieces are more muted and not bold
- Color block by choosing solid colors that compliment your bold pant

> ***"Fashion changes, but style endures." - Coco Chanel***

Build up your wardrobe staples, get inspired and infuse your personal and professional style with those things that are you and reflect your personality. Take your time. You don't have to revamp your style in one day, weekend, or months. You can pick up pieces every so often to keep your wardrobe current. Also, get rid of something if you find that you still have tons of clothing that you never wear. Once you have developed a style that is representative of you then be sure to refine it from time to time and never forget to take pride in your appearance. It could be the thing that gives you a leg up on the competition because your leaders can see you as a person that will represent them well in meetings with potential and current clients. Don't let something that you have 100 percent control over deter you from gaining the confidence of your employers and be a stumbling block on the way to a successful career.

SIMPLY DO:

- **Do take pride in your appearance.**
- **Do invest in quality statement pieces.**
- **Do dress for the job you want.**
- **Do get style inspiration from all things and people that inspire you.**
- **Do declutter your closet by getting rid of items of clothing, shoes, and handbags that you no longer wear.**
- **Do shop around and look for deals.**

Digital Download of the ***Simpli Style Wardrobe Staples*** available at:

https://stacihuddleston.com/secure-success-guides/

15

SIMPLY SERVICE

We make a living by what we get, but we make a life by what we give.

- Winston Churchill

Once you've found a way to prosper both personally and professional you maybe wondering what's next? You have taken care of yourself, you are where you want to be professionally, and the combination of your passion and purpose is bringing you prosperity then it's time to give back.

GIVING BACK

Whether someone helped you along the way or not, it is my belief that you should take the time to help another person reach their full potential by giving of yourself, your time, your talents, and/or your funds. Along the way I've had great role models to show me what a successful person looks like. I've had phenomenal mentors who have coached me throughout my career and have gone the extra mile to make sure I continued to move up professionally and that I was prepared when I got there. Those things are invaluable. There is nothing like being in a position and not having the right tools to succeed when you get there. Trust me, I've been there before, and I still succeeded because I had the wherewithal to teach myself what I needed to know. Be sure to share your time, talents, and tithes as often as you can to be a blessing to someone else.

TALENT

Giving of yourself could be a number of things. In my current career, I've mentored interns who have come after me by imparting the knowledge of what worked and what didn't work as I navigated my professional career over the last decade. As a leader, it is my responsibility to listen to my employees and to allow them to tell me what it is they want to achieve in their careers. Some people are more than happy with doing the least amount of work to get by or just doing a mediocre job in their current roles until they retire. Everyone does not have the same goals. It isn't my job to want something for those individuals that they don't want for themselves, however, it is my responsibility to make sure that if they want to discuss career development or anything else for that matter that my door is always open. I believe that it is my calling to help others to succeed both personally and professionally. My skill set and time are both precious commodities but I believe that it is my duty to give of myself to others to help them succeed as well. It is my every intention to coach and mentor my employees for the careers they want. I strive to encourage and mentor my junior employees and interns throughout their careers. I take the time to review and revise resumes, provide interview prep and mock interviews, as well as encouraging others to take training and to obtain certifications that will be key in helping them to get to where they want to be professionally. Money could also help others realize their dreams and fuel their success. If you have the funds to spare and you truly believe in someone's dreams, then giving back could be investing in their projects or businesses. It could be mutually beneficial if their projects or businesses succeed but it can also be beneficial for your soul to give others a boost in confidence by letting them know that you genuinely believe in them. If no one took the time and opportunity to show you that they believed in your dreams and aspirations, then think of how much you would have appreciated it if they did. This is why we give back because doing for others is also good for you.

Those are some of the ways I give back in the professional arena, but you can give back in a multitude of ways. Are you knowledgeable in the law, medicine, or accounting? How about providing some services pro bono, donating work without charge to those less fortunate who can't afford your services. Teachers? Are there students in your community that can use your tutoring services? How about donating an hour or so a week to giving back by tutoring children whose parents cannot afford to hire a tutor. No matter your profession, skills, or talents, there is something that you can do that can be of help to someone else. A barber offering free or discounted haircuts to children in the neighborhood after hours, or a cosmetologist donating a portion of their time and talents to washing and styling the hair of people in nursing homes are all considered forms of giving back. The things you can do are limitless, you just have to think about what you can do and dedicate some time to actually doing it.

TIME

Say for instance, if you can't find a way to use your particular talents or skillset to provide a service then you can always donate time to helping out at a soup kitchen or shelter feeding the homeless or those who are down on their luck. Donating clothing, toiletries, and many other things to those who do not have can bring you such joy. One of my friends sent out a mass text message asking if anyone wanted to go feed the homeless one Saturday and I said why not? If I were homeless I would definitely want someone to give of their time and resources to help me out.

It really blessed my heart to see all the young ladies of Purposeful Youth Detroit along with their parents, mentors, and other volunteers taking the time on a Saturday afternoon to give to those less fortunate. The feeling is indescribable, but if I had to try, I would say that we all wanted to feed as many people as possible if for one day, they had something good to eat. What was most overwhelming and nearly brought tears of joy to my eyes was the sight of other people setting up food lines down the block from where we were located. In the two hours we were there, we saw three other food lines being set up to feed the homeless as well as a number of cars that pulled up to disburse t-shirts, socks, and pre-made toiletry bags. It really blessed my heart and showed me that I can be doing so much more. There are still good people in this world and I want to be one of them. I recommend you do something, anything you can for someone else in a selfless act like I witnessed that weekend. I guarantee it will not only bless someone else but it will certainly bless you too!

Mentor young girls, single moms, or any demographic you feel led to help. Spend time getting to know them and teaching them from your experiences. Mentoring is a highly rewarding way to give back. Seeing these individuals grow over time and succeed on their own merit will give you a sense of pride since you have witnessed their growth. Most of these relationships are mutually beneficial; the mentors end up learning so much from the mentees even though they weren't expecting to.

TITHES

> *"There are several things to be learned about money from Scripture, and the concepts of generosity and giving are in there." - Dave Ramsey*

When we hear the word tithes, it is most times associated with the 10 percent of everything that you receive should be given back to God or the church in today's society. I was raised in the church and I am a tither. My maternal Grandmother, Betty, taught me about tithing when I was visiting church with her as a young girl. I know that the bible says that I should do so and I will keep it 100% honest with all of you. There were times in my life when I wasn't tithing on a regular basis and I would notice that unexpected things would go wrong in my world costing more than what my initial tithes would have been if I'd paid them to the church. It may sound crazy to some but I do believe God is going to get his regardless. I give the first 10 percent to God, then the next 10 percent to myself in the form of savings, then I live off the rest. Surprisingly, once I started tithing frequently, it seemed like I had more money than when I was being selfish in trying to keep it all for me. I know that everyone isn't a believer and this is not the book where I am going to try to turn you into one, however, my shameless plug for Jesus Christ: if you have not accepted Jesus Christ as your Lord and Savior give it a shot; I don't think you will be disappointed. Now that we've got that out of the way let's get back to it. Giving tithes, offering, money to those less fortunate, non-profit organizations, charities, churches who provide massive support to the community in the form of food, shelter, mental health, medical services to name a few are all ways that you can give back. Honestly, the sky is the limit and you can give as much as you can afford to those individuals, organizations, and causes that are near and dear to your hearts. Most charitable donations can be tax write-offs when you file your taxes, so be sure to keep receipts and records of when you donate and how much you give. Donating clothes and gently used goods to the Salvation Army or Purple Heart are also tax write-offs.

I have a cousin who has taken in many family members over the years while they were in college pursuing higher education out of state. Not only did she work tirelessly helping several people including me from our hometown to gain acceptance into her Alma Matter, Alabama A&M University, she also lent a helping hand and roof while they needed it. I truly benefited from her caring spirit and looking back on it, I've never met a more altruistic person than my cousin, Nikky. She opened her heart and her family's home to help others. One thing she unknowingly taught me was to try harder to be selfless. I've recently been using the connections that I have in my industry to help recent graduates to gain employment after graduation with my employer – notifying them of opportunities, linking them up with someone who can help them curate their resumes and also providing them with interview prep and mock interviews to give them the confidence to perform at their best during the interviews once they are selected for an interview. I didn't realize how gratifying helping others pursue new careers could be until the first one notified me that she'd been selected for a position she'd interviewed for and would be moving from Illinois to Michigan to begin her career. I've since helped my sister through the process as well and she landed a job to jump-start her career two months after graduating from college. I'm not sure how you can help but if you are fortunate enough to do so, please give back in any way that you can.

Digital Download of the ***Simpli Service 5 Ways to Give Back*** available at:

https://stacihuddleston.com/secure-success-guides/

16

SIMPLY SUMMARY

Life isn't about finding yourself. Life is about creating yourself

- Unknown

Success is multi-faceted and if you want to be successful in life you have to make sure that you are making an effort to be the best you that you can be. Never stop trying and putting in 100 percent effort into every area of your life every single day. Imagine the life you want, map out how you will achieve it, and work the plan. There may be some detours along the way but don't lose your focus. Determination and perseverance will help you stay the course. Once you are where you want to be in terms of success, don't forget to reap the benefits of your success. Enjoy the fruits of your labor. Do you want to be your Simply Successful Self living your Best Life EVER? If you answered YES, then my advice to you is, "Don't fade into the background; stand out! Live the life you are destined to live, travel the world, help others, give back, do the things that make you happy, and never stop learning! You have the ability to be the person you desire to be. Live your life in a way that strengthens your character, adds to your happiness, and inspires others! Life is what you make it; so, make it absolutely grand!"

CREATING YOUR ROAD MAP TO SUCCESS

WHAT IS YOUR DEFINITION OF SUCCESS?

Take some time to think about and jot down what success looks like to you. How does it make you feel? What does successful you do on a normal day? How does successful you spend your free time? How does successful you make a living? These are important questions to ask yourself. Successful Staci does something I love and I make money doing it! I spend time with family and friends eating good food, enjoying good libations, and traveling the world! Successful "me" helps others achieve their goals and live the lives they've always envisioned.

ASSESS EACH AREA OF YOUR LIFE...

In order to define what success means to you, you have to take inventory of the current areas of your life to determine if you currently see yourself as being successful in each of these areas:

- **Simply Self**
  - Your beliefs.
  - Your health – mental and physical.
  - Your finances.
- **Simply 'Ships**
  - Your personal relationships.
  - Your professional relationships.
- **Simply Skilled**
  - Your career.

PRIORITIZE AND SET GOALS…

Once you've completed your assessment of what you perceive your level of success to be in each area; and have a better understanding of what being successful in those areas actually looks like to you, it is time to set realistic goals. This will help you to improve and optimize your success in the areas you feel you are coming up a little short in.

Set SMART (specific, measurable, attainable, realistic, and timely) goals to improve the areas of your life that need improving. Prioritize those goals so that you are focusing on the most important ones and not floundering around trying to work them all equally and not making significant headway with any.

REVISIT AND REVISE GOALS...

Take time to revisit and revise goals that no longer serve you. If you've completed any, then readjust and reprioritize the others. Over time, new goals may come up that you need to add to your ongoing list. There will likely always be another goal to accomplish, your list will likely never diminish. However, it is likely that over time your list changes.

MAKE ADJUSTMENTS IN YOUR LIFE TO ACHIEVE THE GOALS YOU'VE SET...

You have to identify what adjustments need to be made and make them. Some things will require discipline and sacrifice. However, as long as you keep your mind on your ultimate goal of being successful in every area of your life, you can continue to manifest the life and level of success you've always envisioned.

ASSESS YOUR PROGRESS AND MAKE THE NECESSARY ADJUSTMENTS ALONG THE WAY...

The road map to success doesn't have an end. Even if you reach that ultimate level of success you've always envisioned, you'll have to continue to work to maintain it. The truth is that the road to success is ongoing and not at all finite.

-Simpli Staci

Digital Download of the ***Creating Your Roadmap to Success Guide*** available at:

https://stacihuddleston.com/secure-success-guides/

BIBLIOGRAPHY

Blatchford, E. (2016, August 22). These Are The Main Reasons Most Couples Fight. Retrieved April 29, 2018, from https://www.huffingtonpost.com.au/2016/08/17/these-are-the-main-reasons-most-couples-fight_a_21453157

DATAUSA. (2014). East St. Louis, IL. Retrieved October 22, 2018, from https://datausa.io/profile/geo/east-st.-louis-il/#intro

Domonell, K. (2016). This Is How Much Exercise You Really Need to Do to See Health Benefits. Retrieved March 16, 2018, from https://www.womenshealthmag.com/fitness/how-much-exercise-you-need-to-do-to-get-health-benefits/slide/5

Duffy, J. (2018, February 08). The Best Personal Finance Services of 2018. Retrieved May 1, 2018, from https://www.pcmag.com/article2/0,2817,2407617,00.asp

Financial Literacy for Everyone. (n.d.-a). Credit Scores. Retrieved June 7, 2018, from https://www.practicalmoneyskills.com/learn/credit/credit_scores

Financial Literacy for Everyone. (n.d.-b). Saving. Retrieved June 6, 2018, from https://www.practicalmoneyskills.com/learn/saving

Kim, N. & Price, G. (n.d.). 22 Affordable Ways to De-stress. Retrieved March 16, 2018, from http://allhealthcare.monster.com/benefits/articles/3671-22-affordable-ways-to-de-stress

Lebowitz, S. (2017, March 04). 12 rich, powerful people share their surprising definitions of success. Retrieved March 04, 2018, from http://www.businessinsider.com/how-successful-people-define-success-2017-3 pp10

Merriam-Webste. (n.d.-a). Networking. Retrieved January 16, 2020, from https://www.merriam-webster.com/dictionary/networking

Merriam-Webster. (n.d.-b). Passion. Retrieved January 16, 2020, from https://www.merriam-webster.com/dictionary/passion

Merriam-Webster. (n.d.-c). Prosperity. Retrieved January 16, 2020, from https://www.merriam-webster.com/dictionary/prosperity

Merriam-Webster. (n.d.-d). Purpose. Retrieved January 16, 2020, from https://www.merriam-webster.com/dictionary/purpose

Mint. (n.d.). Money, Bill Pay, Credit Score & Investing. Retrieved June 6, 2018, from http://www.mint.com

National Alliance on Mental Illness. (n.d.). Self-Care Inventory. Retrieved May 13, 2018, from https://www.nami.org/getattachment/Extranet/Education,-Training-and-Outreach-Programs/Signature-Classes/NAMI-Homefront/HF-Additional-Resources/HF15AR6SelfCare.pdf

Produce for Better Health Foundation. (n.d.). Healthy Meal Planning Guide. Retrieved March 16, 2018, from http://

www.fruitsandveggiesmorematters.org/healthy-meal-planning-guide

Razzetti, G. (2018, February 8). Why Your Success Depends on The Strength of Your Relationships. Retrieved May 2, 2018, from https://medium.com/personal-growth/why-your-success-depends-on-the-strength-of-your-relationships-feed3e17dd0c pp

Weliver, D. (2018, March 22). How Credit Works: Understand Your Credit Report And Score. Retrieved June 6, 2018, from https://www.moneyunder30.com/how-credit-works

ABOUT THE AUTHOR

Staci D. Huddleston is an author, financial coach, former collegiate instructor, and the founder of Simpli Services LLC. Staci has a passion for helping others become the best possible versions of themselves. She believes that anybody can achieve success no matter their background, and through her writing, she hopes to provide readers with practical ways to prosper both personally and professionally by identifying their goals, embracing who they are, and striving to attain their dreams. When not writing or helping people through her professional life, Staci enjoys building memories by traveling the world and adding new countries' stamps to her passport.

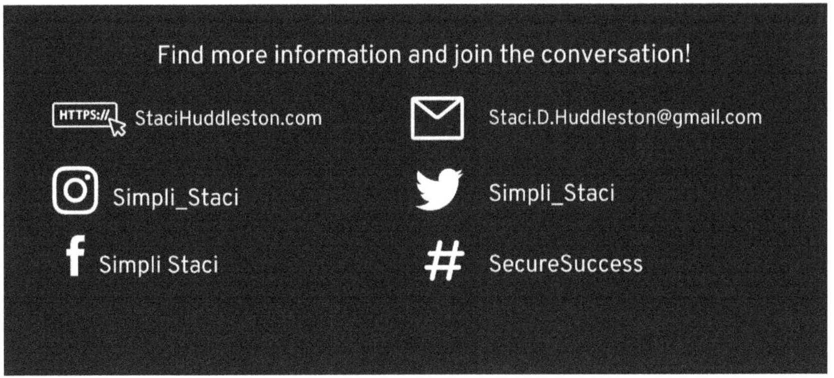

Find more information and join the conversation!
HTTPS://
StaciHuddleston.com
Staci.D.Huddleston@gmail.com
Simpli_Staci
Simpli_Staci
Simpli Staci
#
SecureSuccess

Lightning Source UK Ltd.
Milton Keynes UK
UKHW020832151220
375245UK00004B/812